Theodor Geisel

WHO
WROTE
THAT?

WHO WROTE THAT?

Theodor Geisel

Tanya Dean

Chelsea House Publishers
Philadelphia

CHELSEA HOUSE PUBLISHERS

EDITOR IN CHIEF Sally Cheney
DIRECTOR OF PRODUCTION Kim Shinners
CREATIVE MANAGER Takeshi Takahashi
MANUFACTURING MANAGER Diann Grasse

STAFF FOR THEODOR GEISEL

ASSOCIATE EDITOR Benjamin Kim
PICTURE RESEARCHER Jane Sanders
PRODUCTION ASSISTANT Jaimie Winkler
SERIES AND COVER DESIGNER Keith Trego
LAYOUT 21st Century Publishing and Communications, Inc.

http://www.chelseahouse.com

First Printing

1 3 5 7 9 8 6 4 2

Library of Congress Cataloging-in-Publication Data

Dean, Tanya.
    Theodor Geisel / Tanya Dean.
      p. cm. — (Who wrote that?)
Includes bibliographical references and index.
    ISBN 0-7910-6724-6 (hardcover)
  1. Seuss, Dr.—Juvenile literature. 2. Authors, American—20th century—
Biography—Juvenile literature. 3. Illustrators—United States—Biography—
Juvenile literature. 4. Children's literature—Authorship—Juvenile literature.
I. Title. II. Series.
PS3513.E2 Z64 2002
813' .52—dc21

                                                2002000166

Table of Contents

Theodor Geisel in 1955. Though he became one of the most famous children's authors and illustrators, his lucky break came when, after getting rejected by 27 publishers, he accidentally ran into a fellow Dartmouth classmate from New York City on the street.

1

To Think That It Happened on Madison Avenue

FEW COUPLES HAD traveled as extensively as Ted and Helen Geisel in their nine years of marriage. Ted, born Theodor Seuss Geisel, was thirty-two years old in 1936, and he was restless. He had found considerable success in his advertising career, but somehow still felt that he was not doing what made him happiest. Enormously talented as both a writer and illustrator, Ted was in demand to create catchy ads that attracted consumers to buy such things as bug spray, fingernail clippers, and automobiles. He was also beginning to find success in drawing cartoons for adults. Frequent travel to Europe was possible because of his successes. Ted and Helen enjoyed these trips, and Ted found that exploring other countries boosted his creativity.

The Geisels boarded the Swedish luxury liner *M.S. Kungsholm* in New York Harbor and headed for Europe in the summer of 1936. An air of uncertainty traveled with the people on board because rumors of possible German aggression in Europe was growing. World War I had ended in 1918, but the tension between Germany, France, and England had not diminished over the years. Instead, the rise of the Nazi Party under the leadership of Adolf Hitler in Germany added to Europeans' fears. Ted, himself a second-generation German-American, was interested in national and international issues and therefore kept a keen eye on these events. Regardless, he and Helen had decided to go ahead with their trip, joining other Americans who also had ventured into Europe that summer to attend the Olympic Summer Games in Berlin. The Geisels did not go to Berlin, but they kept up on the news of Jesse Owens's four gold medals as they dined at Swiss cafés.

Ted enjoyed the Swiss scenery—the pointed mountains, the winding roads, the unusual buses and houses. Here his imagination could come alive again. He drew scenes of odd creatures hanging from dangerous peaks or wandering up long, crooked paths. Just for fun, he learned to yodel. Helen, while encouraging, suggested he keep practicing—but only in the shower.

By the time their holiday was nearly over, the threat of invasion by Hitler was more imminent. Ted was concerned about his grandfather's homeland, and indeed all of Europe, and he told Helen perhaps it was time for him to get serious about his own life. She knew that it was her husband's deepest longing to write and draw his own children's books. Even though Ted had enjoyed illustrating someone else's stories a few years earlier (*Boners* in 1931), Helen suggested that he should go ahead and try his hand at writing his own children's book. Ted agreed.

The Geisels boarded the *M.S. Kungsholm* for home, eager to return with a new plan in mind. They had been aboard for only eight days, however, when a powerful storm pounded the ship. Helen stayed in her cabin during the worst hours, but Ted grew anxious and needed to move around. He held on tightly to the rails as he walked the deck, but eventually gave up his pacing and sat down at the ship's bar. There he picked up some of the ship's stationery and began to write. The rhythm of the ship's engines ran through his mind, over and over again, and the mixture of the incessant beat and the bouncy ride on rough seas made concentration difficult. To settle his mind, Ted began to recite lines from "'Twas the Night Before Christmas," which, oddly enough, seemed to match the rhythm of the engine sounds. Then, seemingly from nowhere, Ted heard and spoke the line, "And that is a story that no one can beat, and to think that I saw it on Mulberry Street." Mulberry Street was, in fact, a real street in his hometown of Springfield, Massachusetts.

Even after Ted and Helen had returned to their home, the young writer could not get the rhythm out of his head. In order to get it to stop, Ted decided to go ahead and write an entire story using that maddening rhythm. If nothing else, perhaps the sounds would go away.

Like most writers, Ted found that finding the words

Hillary Clinton reading a Dr. Seuss book to pre-school children in Milwaukee. The popularity of his books with schoolchildren continues to this day.

that were "just right" for his story was not easy. He wrote, rewrote, and kept rewriting the manuscript, always critical of his own choice of words. More than anything, he wanted to write and illustrate a book that would make children want "to turn page after page," as he told Helen.

Ted drew illustrations to help fill out the story, making creatures and scenes that would delight and tell the story all by themselves. Although some writers in the 1930s preferred to use a typewriter when writing a manuscript, Ted preferred to print with pencil on yellow paper. Six months after beginning, Ted completed the book he entitled *A Story That No One Can Beat,* a book filled with odd creatures and characters creating their own parade on Mulberry Street.

Nowadays when a writer or illustrator wants to submit something to a publisher, he or she usually will use the U.S. mail or another delivery service to send the material. In the 1930s and 40s, however, it was not unusual for people to actually carry their manuscripts or drawings from publisher to publisher in New York City. That is

Did you know...

When *And to Think That I Saw It on Mulberry Street* became available to the public in 1937, the people of Springfield, Massachusetts, were a little concerned. Unsure of what the book was really about, some townspeople were afraid that the book was going to tell personal, even embarrassing, stories about some of them who actually lived on Mulberry Street. Imagine their relief when they finally saw Dr. Seuss's children's book. Instead of a serious tattle-telling book, *Mulberry Street* delighted them with tons of funny-looking creatures and a little boy who had a great imagination . . . a boy like the Ted Geisel they had known.

exactly what Ted Geisel did. During the winter of 1936-37, he showed his book to twenty-seven different publishers. One after one, they rejected *A Story That No One Can Beat*, often commenting that it was "too different" from the kinds of children's books being developed at the time. Few rhyming books were being published, and the odd illustrations Ted had drawn were even more atypical. Some publishers even complained that his story had no moral or lesson for the child. Ted was especially upset about that criticism. He had not intended to preach to children; instead, he merely had wanted to give them something fun to read.

The twenty-seventh rejection was the last one for Ted. Dejected, he shoved the papers under his arm and decided to do two things: to return to his advertising and cartoon work for adults and to burn his only copy of *A Story That No One Can Beat*. He headed for home, walking along Madison Avenue in New York City. Lost in thought, Ted was surprised to hear his name called by a familiar voice. It was Mike McClintock, a fellow classmate of his from his college years at Dartmouth. Right away, Mike asked Ted what he had under his arm. Ted answered that it was a children's book manuscript that he was taking home to burn because no one was interested in publishing it. Mike smiled at Ted and pointed at the building in front of which they were standing. Ted's old friend had just been hired, only three hours previously, as the juvenile book editor at that particular publishing house, Vanguard Press. He invited Ted to come up to his office so they could take a look at the book he was getting ready to destroy.

Thirty minutes later, Vanguard Press's publisher James Henle agreed to publish the book. The only immediate change he wanted involved the title. Henle felt that the book needed a catchier title in order to sell successfully. Henle was different from most publishers of that time because he was interested in making books that no one else was making yet. He was willing to take some risks by publishing new kinds of books by new authors and illustrators. Ted's second title was the one that stuck: *And to Think That I Saw It on Mulberry Street.* About that lucky day, Ted later told people, "If I had been going down the other side of Madison Avenue, I'd be in the dry-cleaning business today." Showing his gratitude, Ted named the story's narrator "Marco," the name of Mike McClintock's son, and he dedicated the book to Mike's wife Helene.

When the book arrived in bookstores in the fall of 1937, James Henle paid for a full-page ad in *Publishers Weekly* magazine, a special magazine for people in the bookselling and publishing business. The ad showed a reindeer pulling a cart down Mulberry Street and read: "Booksellers, hitch on! This is the start of a parade that will take you places!" by "the good Dr. Seuss." Ted had used the pseudonym "Dr. Seuss" since his college days, and he wanted to continue to use it on his children's books, too. (A pseudonym is a "pen name" some authors use instead of their real name.) He sometimes commented, less-than-seriously, that he was saving his "real" name for his first novel.

The book reviews about *Mulberry Street* were positive from the beginning. One of the first reviews helped establish Dr. Seuss as one of the best children's book authors of his time. It simply said, "They say it's for children, but better get a copy for yourself and marvel at the good Dr. Seuss' impossible pictures and the moral

The curtain call from the Broadway show called "Seussical," a musical celebration of the Dr. Seuss books with characters such as the Cat in the Hat (played by Rosie O' Donnell), Horton (played by Kevin Chamberlin) and Gertrude McFuzz (played by Jenny Hill).

tale of a little boy who exaggerated . . . " Another reviewer described the book as being a mix of "the funny papers and the tall tale."

Mulberry Street was colorful and expensive to print, but despite the one-dollar cover price (which was expensive for a children's book at that time), it sold even better than the publisher had expected. Dr. Seuss had landed on bookshelves and in the hearts of adults and children all over the country.

Springfield, Massachusetts, where Theodor Geisel was born and raised.

2

Dr. Seuss Learns His ABCs

THEODOR SEUSS GEISEL was born on March 2, 1904, in Springfield, Massachusetts to Theodor Robert Geisel and Henrietta Seuss Geisel. His parents from the beginning called him Ted. Little Ted joined an older sister, Margaretha Christine Geisel, who also decided to shorten her long name. A fun-loving and intelligent girl, she often told people her name was "Marnie Mecca Ding Ding Guy." From that came the name everyone called her: Marnie. Ted, only two years younger, adored her.

The Geisels were among the nearly one thousand German-Americans who lived in Springfield, and Ted's grandfather (also named Theodor Geisel) was co-owner of one of the most successful businesses in town, a brewery. Springfield, Massachusetts, was already well-known for three landmark companies: the Smith and Wesson gun business; the Milton Bradley game company; and G. and C. Merriam, publishers of the nation's best-known dictionary. Ted's grandfather had immigrated from Muhlhausen, Germany, to the United States, settling in Springfield, in 1867. The Kalmbach and Geisel Brewery opened in 1876. The townspeople nick-named it the "come back and guzzle" brewery. Both the Geisel family and the Kalmbach family lived next to the business. In 1879, Ted's father was born in Springfield. It was a good city for a growing business and a loving family.

Ted's mother, Henrietta (Nettie) Seuss, also was born and grew up in this town. Her parents had immigrated there from the Bavarian region of Germany, and they pronounced their last name as it had been in Germany: *zoice,* not *zoos*. The Geisel family business made beer, and the Seuss family business made bread. When the young Theodor Geisel married the baker's daughter, some townspeople made it their business to criticize both families. At the turn of the century, owning a bakery was an admirable business venture; however, owning a brewery was not. Concerns over excessive drinking caused political reformers to think that they should make the purchase of alcohol illegal. This idea turned into the Prohibition movement, whose leaders wanted to stop the production, sale, and distribution of alcohol in the United States.

In 1901, when Ted's parents got married, the Prohibition movement was already well underway. The most vocal group was the Women's Christian Temperance Union. They (and others) believed that drinking alcohol was a special problem in our country, harming individuals, families, and communities. At first, it was up to individual states to pass laws that would make their own state "dry," meaning it was illegal to sell or buy alcohol. (Even today, some communities are still "dry.") Eventually, however, reformers wanted the federal government to establish an amendment to the Constitution that would make prohibition the law of the land. In 1920, the Eighteenth Amendment did just that. For twenty years, the Kalmbach and Geisel Brewery suffered year by year as this movement grew. Eventually it closed and Ted's father had to find new work to support his family.

Ted grew up knowing all about the tensions regarding his grandfather's business, but he had a happy childhood nonetheless. Nettie read bedtime stories to her son and daughter, using a soft, rhythmic voice to lull them to sleep. Ted often told others that his mother was the one who had helped set the rhythms in his mind that he used when writing children's books. Nettie Geisel nurtured Ted's love of words by reading books that were imaginative. One of Ted's favorites was *The Hole Book* by Peter Newell. Each page actually had a hole in it. This was the first book that made Ted think that writing children's book could be fun. His mother also read rhyming books to Ted and Marnie, particularly the *Goops* books by Gelett Burgess. As Ted grew older, Nettie knew that she could get him to do things he didn't really want to do just by promising to buy him a book. Ted agreed to take piano lessons, for example, when he learned he could get books for playing well.

Ted's father was loving, too, and provided the discipline that would be so important in the writer's life. From his father Ted learned to strive to do the very best he could. The elder Geisel was an expert marksman who held a world title in 1902. He tried to teach Ted to shoot, too, but Ted was not quite as good as his father. Still, he learned what it took to "hit the target," not only in this sport but in his other endeavors as well.

Ted and Marnie loved to play in and around their house on Fairfield Street. The attic held trunks filled with all kinds of clothing. Ted and Marnie would dress up in costumes and pretend to be all kinds of people and things. Ted was especially fond of wearing hats, something he would continue to enjoy to the end of his life. His room was littered with books, paper, and pencils, as doodling was one of his favorite pastimes. The young Geisels could hear the sounds of the animals at the nearby Springfield Zoo, one of their favorite places to visit. Although Ted regularly saw the real animals, he would draw them as funny-looking creatures. He often included them in his silly stories and cartoons.

Growing up in Springfield, Massachusetts was mostly a wonderful experience for Ted. Two incidents were not pleasant, however. Another sister, Henrietta, was born in 1906 and died of pneumonia eighteen months later. Ted never forgot seeing her tiny casket as it rested in the music room of his house. He also never forgot being locked in a closet as punishment for "bad behavior" by their house-keeper. From that time on, Ted became *claustrophobic*— afraid of small, enclosed spaces. Even as an adult, he was unable to overcome this fear.

Ted Geisel started school in 1908. He loved to watch the goings-on along the streets of Springfield: the horse-drawn wagons, the trolley cars, bicycles, and the auto-mobiles that bumped along. Ted played with classmates and earned their friendship because of his easygoing ways. He loved to laugh and smile, and he told the best stories around. Though he was not very athletic, Ted had other strengths that made him well-liked and popular. He was, for instance, the winner of his friends' ear-wiggling contest. Some of these early friends would show up in some of Dr. Seuss's books later. These buddies had some unusual names, like Norval Bacon, and Ted loved to name his characters accordingly. Words were magical to Ted, and he seldom passed up an opportunity to tuck away a word or name in his memory for later use.

Ted and his father enjoyed a close friendship. When Mr. Geisel was appointed to the Springfield Park board in 1909, he began to take Ted on walks through the beautiful park and behind the scenes at the park's centerpiece: the Springfield Zoo. Ted brought along his sketchbook and drew pictures of plants and animals that he saw. Of course, Ted's pictures seldom looked like the real thing, and his sister loved to tease him about his odd drawings.

Did you know...

Dr. Seuss made up the names of most of his animal creatures. In fact, he said he had a special dictionary he used to look up the spellings. However, when it came to naming people in his stories, this fun-loving author often used the names of real people he knew or had known. For example, Marco (*And to Think That I Saw It on Mulberry Street* and *McElligot's Pool*) was named for the son of his publisher, Mike McClintock. The lovable elephant Horton (*Horton Hatches the Egg* and *Horton Hears a Who!*) was named for a classmate at Dartmouth College.

Ted's Springfield roots continue even after his death. In 2001, Representative Paul Caron of Springfield, Massachusetts argued for making Theodor Geisel the official children's author of Massachusetts.

Mr. Geisel later recalled that "Ted always had a pencil in hand." Just as Mrs. Geisel encouraged Ted's love of words, Mr. Geisel supported his son's drawing talents. Their mutual love of nature grew, too. In 1910, father and son sat in a field behind their house to wait for the appearance of Halley's Comet, a phenomenon that happens only every 76 years. Ted recalled that "I saw Halley's Comet and my first owl on the same night."

At the end of each workday, Mr. Geisel was met at the corner by Ted, who knew his father had brought him a copy of the daily *Boston American* newspaper. Ted's favorite part was the comic page, and his favorite comic strip was *Krazy Kat*. The two Geisel men especially enjoyed spending time in the workshop Ted's father had set up. Together they tinkered and invented things, such as a "biceps-strengthening machine." Ted loved to see other Springfielders' inventions, too, and he copied advertisements he saw in the newspaper of such inventions as a new coal stove with a complex maze of compartments. Ted loved things that had intricate looping sections or wild, winding stairs. These kinds of objects eventually found their way into his books.

Ted recalled many historical events that took place when he lived in Springfield. He was ten years old when he saw the headlines announcing the sinking of the great luxury liner *RMS Titanic*. He wrote a poem about the event. He was excited to read about the opening of the Panama Canal in 1914, and this "shortcut" made Ted eager to travel. This remarkable man-made canal across Central America would allow ships to cut across the middle of the Western Hemisphere rather than having to travel all the way around the tip of South America.

The Geisels experienced long-distance technology first-hand as well. In 1915, Mr. and Mrs. Geisel decided to travel to San Francisco by train to attend the World's Fair. Ted's father made his family proud when he took part in a demonstration at one of the fair's booths. The operators of the booth invited him to call any city in the country. Few places had telephones in 1915, and transcontinental phone calls were practically unheard of. Local calls were more common instead. So Ted's father called the mayor of Springfield, Massachusetts! Ted never forgot the headlines in the next day's newspaper: GEISEL CALLS MAYOR.

Ted grew up knowing and appreciating his German heritage. He and Marnie even spoke German before they spoke English. They sang Christmas songs in their native language and practiced German traditions. In the early twentieth century, many Americans were closely connected to their European cultures and were proud of who they were. As Ted became a teenager, however, the mood of the country was changing. Eleven-year-old Ted was shocked along with the rest of America to hear of the attack against the British ocean liner *Lusitania* in 1915. The Germans had torpedoed the ship. It sank, and among the nearly 1,200 who died were 128 Americans. Even in small towns like Springfield, German-Americans suffered insults and cold stares. As World War I drew near, Ted could see the changes around him, but he did not understand people's prejudices. He did not want to be treated like a lesser person because of his heritage. Although it hurt to see fellow German-Americans come under suspicion, Ted covered his concern and pain with his ready smile and outgoing sense of humor.

Ted turned thirteen in 1917, and the country was entering a new era. Not only was Prohibition on the horizon—and with it the certainty that the Geisel's business would have to close—but it was also becoming clear that the U.S. would soon be joining the war in Europe. Many German-Americans had mixed feelings about this—they loved their homeland but they valued their new home here, too. In April 1917, the German navy attacked American ships on the seas and President Wilson declared war on Germany. From this point on, the Geisel

The Lusitania. *Its 1915 sinking at the hands of a German torpedo was another event that would arouse suspicion of German-Americans like Ted and his family.*

family knew that thinking of itself as German-American was not wise. Indeed, the Geisel clan was an American family, actively involved on the home front in providing support for the war effort. Mrs. Geisel and Marnie knitted socks and afghans for the troops. Ted sold Liberty Bonds, the primary way the government raised money during the war. In fact, he sold so many that in 1918 he was among a group of Boy Scouts to receive a medal from former president Theodore Roosevelt. Sadly, this event turned out to be a disappointment for fourteen-year-old Ted. When the former president had handed out the last medal, Ted stood alone, still waiting for his. Someone had made a mistake and had ordered nine instead of ten medals. Ted felt foolish and embarrassed as President Roosevelt asked him, "What are you doing here?" He had no answer. From that moment on, Ted Geisel would harbor a fear of making public appearances.

The war ended in November 1918 when Ted was a sophomore at Central High School. Ted took his only formal art class there and soon transferred out. He was frustrated by all the rules the art teacher imposed about the "right way" to draw things. Later, the man who would be known as Dr. Seuss said, "I was free forever from art-by-the-rule books. . . . That teacher wanted me to draw the world as it is, and I wanted to draw things as I saw them." The teacher's suggestion that Ted consider finding another career besides art only made the young man more determined someday to make his living as an artist. In his other classes, Ted was a B-student, except in math, which was very hard for him. He enjoyed school, especially the extracurricular activities, and found a place for his humor, writing, and drawing skills at *The Recorder,* the school's weekly newspaper. Ted drew cartoons and wrote humorous one-liners, poems, and satires, usually under the pseudonym T. S. LeSieg (Geisel spelled backwards). As a senior, he was joke editor of the yearbook, had a part in the senior play, and was secretary of the student senate. His class voted him Class Artist and Class Wit.

Of all his teachers at Central High School, only one saw how truly talented Ted Geisel was. Edwin "Red" Smith was a recent graduate of Dartmouth and became

Ted's English teacher at CHS. This teacher made Ted believe that he really could make a living as a writer and illustrator. Mr. Smith encouraged Ted to apply to Dartmouth, where many of Ted's classmates were headed, and he wrote a letter of recommendation that secured Ted's acceptance to the university. In June 1921, Theodor Seuss Geisel graduated high school and looked forward to his college years at Dartmouth.

Dartmouth College, where Ted went to college. Here he would write and illustrate for various school publications, beginning his career in earnest.

3

The Grad Becomes an Ad Man

IN 1921, TED started college at Dartmouth in Hanover, Connecticut. The new decade brought the Geisel family some difficult financial times. When Prohibition finally was passed as the Eighteenth Amendment in 1920, the family-owned brewery had to be shut down. Grandfather Geisel had passed away during Ted's senior year of high school, so Ted's father had become president of the brewery. With the brewery closed (and unlikely to ever reopen), Mr. Geisel had to look for other work. During Ted's college years, his father found some success in the real estate business. He continued to serve on the park's board, but without any income. Thankfully, an inheritance from Ted's grandfather made it possible for Ted to continue with his plans for a college education.

Ted wanted to major in English. He loved writing and literature and looked forward to his classes. During his first semester at Dartmouth, Ted wanted to write for the college's humor magazine, *Jack-O-Lantern. Jacko*, as it was called by the students, became Ted's passion, much more than his classes. He drew cartoons, usually signing them "Ted G.," and wrote some funny one-liners. Ted always wore a bow tie. This became his trademark for the rest of his life. Classmates saw a young man who always smiled, often joked, and was never mean-spirited toward anyone. "You never heard him grump," said one classmate.

Ted enjoyed taking classes in German and German literature. Some of his other favorite classes included botany, zoology, and the psychology of advertising. All of those classes would prove useful later. He learned which colors people pay the most attention to, such as red. Ted usually carried a sketchbook to class so he could draw. He drew plants and animals, but he seldom stopped there. Some objects looked "normal," but many were more than a little unusual. Once he drew a picture of his zoology professor's dog, a beagle named Spot. It was a good likeness of Spot, except that Ted had drawn the dog with antlers coming out of his head. Would this creature later reappear as the Grinch's best friend Max?

Ted continued to write and draw for *Jacko*. Many students and faculty recognized his work, making him quite popular. As a sophomore and junior, he spent most of his time at *Jacko's* office. His editor-in-chief at *Jacko* was a young man named Norman Maclean, who later wrote the story that became the feature film *A River Runs Through It*. Ted himself became editor-in-chief his senior year. Here Ted learned how to make words and pictures work together to say something—something silly or something important. He also learned to use pseudonyms to keep some people from knowing which cartoons he'd drawn. Some of these made-up names included Sing Sing Prison, L. Burbank, and Seuss.

When graduation day approached, Ted decided he wanted like to attend Oxford University in England. Ted applied for a fellowship there, knowing his family did not have the money to pay for such a costly education. A fellowship is a kind of scholarship for graduate school. Before even hearing if he'd been awarded it or not, Ted exaggerated by telling his father that the fellowship was his. The next day, after his proud father had shared the news with the editor of the town's newspaper, everyone had heard of Ted's "good fortune." Unfortunately, Ted did not get the fellowship. He waited until graduation day to tell his father the bad news. Mr. Geisel gave Ted a strong stare. A proud man, Mr. Geisel said that since the newspaper had reported that Ted was going to go to Oxford, then the family just would have to make a way. In August 1925, Ted Geisel sailed for England.

Ted's stay at Oxford was short but memorable. At first, he thought he wanted to become a professor of English literature. A few classes taught him that he really did *not* want to teach. World War I had ended only a few years earlier, and Ted's German ancestry made him feel as if he were an outsider. He found other "outsiders" to socialize with. His humorous writings and never-ending sketches kept him company, too. Ted bordered his literature notes with characters that would someday be famous. One of his new friends, an American girl named Helen Palmer, watched as he doodled in class. She loved his illustrations, particularly one of a flying cow. She told him, "You're crazy to be a professor. What you really want to do is draw." About the two students' attraction, Ted later remarked, "You never saw a better case of love at first sight."

Ted and his encouraging classmate Helen became inseparable, and often rode together on a motorcycle with a sidecar. During one trip, Ted accidentally ran off the road and he and Helen ended up in a ditch. They were unharmed, but Ted took that opportunity to ask Helen to marry him. Picking grass from her hair, she accepted.

Although Ted was happy with Helen as his fianceé, he was not happy with school at Oxford. One of his college advisors suggested he leave the classroom and travel through Europe instead. That would be an education all its own. Helen finished her master's degree and planned to return to the U.S. to teach English. In 1926, after her schooling was over, she did just that. Ted spent the summer touring Europe with his family, who had come to visit him. The Geisels traveled in Germany, England, France, and Switzerland. After Mr. and Mrs. Geisel and Marnie returned to Massachusetts, Ted went back to Paris to study. Soon the young man realized he did not know enough French to understand what his teachers were saying. While in Paris, Ted saw a few well-known American writers, including Ernest Hemingway. "I was scared . . . to walk over and ask him [what he was writing] lest he ask me what *I* was writing. I was a twenty-two-year-old kid writing knock-kneed limericks about goats and geese and other stuff that I couldn't sell. He was probably writing *A Farewell to Arms*."

Realizing that his formal education was over, Ted got on a boat and went to the island of Corsica off the coast of France. He painted pictures of donkeys for a month. When he felt his drawing was not going well, he tried writing again. He even tried to write a novel in Italian—and he knew even less Italian than he knew French. "I couldn't understand a word of it," he later said. Ted did not waste his creativity, though—he turned the entire chapter into one two-line cartoon.

Ted returned home to the United States in February 1927. Helen had already arrived a month earlier to accept a teaching position in Orange, New Jersey, not far from New York City. Ted's ship docked at New York Harbor and Helen met him there. Ted had no job leads, so their marriage plans would have to wait. After a nice dinner, Ted said good-bye to Helen as he boarded a train for Springfield to join his family.

Eager to get a start as a freelance writer and illustrator, Ted set up an office at his Fairfield Street home. He sent off dozens of cartoons and humorous writings to publishers in New York, hoping one of them would buy his work or offer him a job. Odd-looking animals and unrecognizable creatures appeared, as usual, in his cartoons. February passed, then March, and then April with no positive responses. Only slightly discouraged, Ted checked into a hotel in New York so he could show his work in person. Helen kept encouraging him and told people about Ted's wonderful animals. But after a week had passed without selling a single thing, Ted returned to Springfield. He drifted in and out of some "funks and depressions," as he called them, but turned his moods into silliness as he created more and more cartoons. This became a pattern of his throughout his life.

Ted started to draw hysterical political cartoons, making fun of some of New York's and Chicago's best-known citizens and leaders. He sent those and other pieces to *Life* magazine, *The Saturday Evening Post,* and *The New Yorker* in particular. May passed, then June. But finally, July brought more than warmth and sunshine—it also brought Ted a letter from *The Saturday Evening Post.* Inside was an acceptance letter and a check for twenty-five dollars for one of his cartoons, which appeared on July 16, 1927. Ted had simply signed it "Seuss." The editors thought that pseudonym was fine, but added in smaller type beneath, "Drawn by Theodor Seuss Geisel." It was his first broadly published work, as readers all over the country subscribed to *The Post.*

Typically optimistic, Ted took his life savings of one thousand dollars and left Springfield for New York City. He and a former staff member of *Jack-O-Lantern* roomed together in rat-infested apartment in Greenwich Village. His roommate, John Rose, knew an editor at a well-known humor magazine called *Judge.* He set Ted up with an interview there. After one interview, Ted was offered a staff position making seventy-five dollars a week. Once again, Ted's positive outlook paid off. Now that he had a good job, Ted was ready to marry Helen. First they had to wait for the birth of Ted's niece. His sister Marnie gave birth to Peggy on November 1, 1927. She became one of Ted's greatest delights. Little Peggy attended Ted and Helen's wedding on November 29, along with about forty other family members and friends. Ted was twenty-three; his bride was twenty-nine.

Ted's work at *Judge* went well, but competition was strong. Magazines depended on advertisements for a large part of their income. (They still do.) Before television

Ted and Helen Geisel. The two met at Oxford and married in 1927.

was a common household item, most ads were in print or on the radio. When buying advertising space in a magazine, a company would decide which magazine to use based on the number of copies sold. *The New Yorker* was *Judge's* fiercest competitor. *The New Yorker* was selling more copies as time went by and pulled some of *Judge's* advertising accounts away. As a result, Ted's salary was reduced to fifty dollars a week. Sometimes he received goods instead of money when things got really tight. For example, one week Ted's salary was 1,872 Little Gem Nail Clippers, care of the company that advertised them in the magazine. Another time he received 100 cans of Barbasol shaving cream. Ted took it in stride, saying "I sort of loved trading my stuff for their stuff. I was happier in one way under the barter system than I've ever been since. When you get paid in money, it leads to accountants and lawyers."

Not only was he published in *Judge,* but he also sold work (for real money) to *Life, Redbook,* and *Vanity Fair.* During this time, Ted began using the pseudonym "Dr. Seuss" for his regular *Judge* feature called "Boids and Beasties." This animal-based cartoon mixed fact and fiction, but usually was heavily weighted toward the fiction side—and Ted's silliness. He thought adding the formal "Dr." to his name made the signature look more professional. He quipped that he saved his father a lot of money by becoming a doctor without going to medical school.

Ted accidentally discovered that interesting things could happen if he used the name of a real product in one of his cartoons. A soda-water bottling company sent him four dozen bottles of soda water after he used the brand name in a cartoon. In the summer of 1928, Ted had an idea for a cartoon about the peskiness of bugs. In those days, people used a spraygun filled with insecticide to keep mosquitoes, flies, and other pests away during the heat of summer. Ted drew a picture of a dragon flying above a knight. The knight was saying, "Darn it all, another Dragon. And just after I'd sprayed the whole castle with Flit!" At the time, Ted flipped a coin to decide whether to use the brand name "Flit" or its competitor, "Fly-Tox." As it happened, "Flit" won out. The wife of an advertising executive for Flit saw the ad while getting her hair done one day. She showed it to her husband and he contacted Ted right away. That single cartoon (helped by the flip of a coin) landed Ted a seventeen-year relationship as cartoonist for Flit. One of Ted's phrases was used over and over, though his drawings changed. Each time the cartoon read: "Quick, Henry, the Flit!" The ad appeared in magazines, on bill-boards, in newspapers, and even in the subway, and sales of Flit increased dramatically. From that account alone, Ted earned twelve thousand dollars a year, a large income at the time. Everyone loved the ads, though some people thought that Ted's bugs were almost too lovable to spray with insecticide.

While most of the 1920s was a time of wealth and prosperity for the country, the last year of the decade brought financial trouble. On October 4, 1929, known as "Black Thursday," the stock market crashed. In the 1920s people had invested a lot of money in the stock market because the price of each share of stock generally kept rising. For example, RCA (Radio Corporation of America) had an all-time high of $505 per share on September 3, 1929. After the Great Stock Market Crash, however, RCA stock tumbled to $28 per share. The Great Depression had begun, and it would last for ten years.

Luckily, Ted and Helen did not suffer the same losses that many other Americans did. Still, Ted worried about the homeless, jobless Americans and was upset that he could do nothing to help "all these people who have nowhere to go." Ted's father continued to work as superintendent

Did you know...

Several of Dr. Seuss's famous animals first appeared on magazine covers, in advertisements, or in cartoons. The March 23, 1929 cover of *Judge* magazine featured two lovable creatures. A kind-looking elephant, jumping over a big hippopotamus, bears a strong resemblance to Horton, the loyal egg-hatcher. Also on that cover was a turtle sitting high atop a tree. Could that be the beginning of Yertle the Turtle? Besides these much-loved critters, Ted Geisel drew lumpy reindeer, super-long-necked giraffes, awkward birds, grinning monkeys, and sleepy-eyed bears. No doubt his childhood years at the Springfield Zoo helped Dr. Seuss create all the animals needed to populate his silly books.

of the park, and Ted was glad of that. Tragically, however, Ted's mother Henrietta Geisel died in March 1931. It was one of the saddest days in Ted's life.

Ted Geisel, a.k.a. Dr. Seuss, kept busy over the next several years, drawing and selling more advertisements. His first book opportunity came in 1931 when an editor at Viking Press asked him to illustrate a book of children's funny sayings. The funny words came from children's school papers in England. In the U.S. the book was called *Boners*. (It was called *Schoolboy Howlers* in England.) It sold so well that a sequel, *More Boners*, was published later the same year.

Ted's illustrations received positive reviews. Ted decided he wanted to write and illustrate his own children's book, an ABC book filled with strange animals. However, no one was interested in his outlandish, bright-colored book. He put it aside when he and Helen became busy moving into a nicer home where Ted set up a studio. After a while, he and Helen began to travel extensively. Ted always took a sketch pad with him when he traveled—and once it was filled, he used hotel stationery. But Ted's love of children's books was not gone for good. Soon his off-the-wall ideas ignited his imagination again.

Ted working on sketches. He would lay out his own pages instead of letting his publishing company's editors and designers dictate the look of his books.

4

Dr. Seuss Hears a "Yes!"

AT A TIME when many Americans had to pinch their pennies, Ted and Helen Geisel were able to travel to Europe, Latin America, and the Middle East. In some ways, these trips were more than vacations for Ted; he needed the stimulation of new places and new people in order to keep his creativity going. Never was this more true than on the *M.S. Kungsholm*, bound for Europe in the summer of 1936. The Geisels' time there (and especially their storm-ridden trip home) was just the right experience at just the right time for Ted to launch his children's book career.

Within a few months, *And to Think That I Saw It on Mulberry Street* was on its way to be printed and bound into the books that would delight children and adults alike. Few authors have the immediate welcome that "Dr. Seuss" had. Reviewers loved the new style of his writing, not to mention the zany drawings that made the stories especially unusual. Vanguard Press, the book's publisher, ordered 15,000 copies to be printed (a one-time printing is called a print run). Even by today's standards, 15,000 is a large print run. Two years later, a second printing of 6,000 copies was made. Even so, it did not look as if Ted was going to get rich by writing and illustrating children's books. An author is often paid a percentage of the sales of his or her book, known as a royalty. In 1937, Dr. Seuss's *Mulberry Street* sold for one dollar. Even if he earned 10 percent as a royalty (and this is a good percentage for a royalty), that means he would earn only 10 cents for each book sold. In that case, the first print run would have earned the good Dr. Seuss only $1,500. In fact, by 1943, he had earned only $3,500 from *Mulberry Street*. What was Ted's solution? To write more books! Helen, who knew him best, knew he was captivated by the fun of creating children's books. As she once said of Ted, "His mind has never grown up."

Ted's childhood love of costumes never grew up either. One day while visiting Ted and Helen, Ted's sister Marnie found that her brother had collected hundreds of hats, including some very old and very weird ones. He told her that he liked to use them to entertain his friends when they came over for dinner. He had a fireman's hat, old helmets, admirals' hats—anything big and heavily decorated. These hats became important as he started his next book, *The 500 Hats of Bartholomew Cubbins.* Unlike *Mulberry Street,* this book did not use lines that rhymed. Instead, it was written in prose, as a fairy tale. Ted got his idea for the book while riding the train from Springfield to New York one day. A gentleman in front of him caught Ted's attention. "He had a real ridiculous Wall Street broker's hat on—very stuffy. And I just began playing around with the idea of what his reaction would be if I took his hat off and threw it out the window. I decided that he was so stuffy that he'd probably grow another one." So Bartholomew Cubbins ended up with the same problem: hats that kept growing from his head. When Ted started writing the story, Bartholomew had

Did you know...

Authors and illustrators often are asked to speak to groups or to sign copies of their books. Ted Geisel, or Dr. Seuss, loved the idea! Unfortunately, he struggled with stage fright most of his life. One day when he was supposed to speak to a group of 300 third-graders, Ted got nervous. He drew and drew, all over the chalkboard. His funny animals appeared here, there, and everywhere. Confident he finally had something to talk about, he asked the children if they liked his drawings. "No," they answered. "Gus [a fellow student] can draw better." Dr. Seuss gave Gus a piece of chalk and had him draw something. When the boy was finished, Dr. Seuss told the students they were right—Gus *could* draw better!

only 48 hats, then he gave him 135, and eventually was satisfied when he'd made the number an even 500. *The 500 Hats* came out in 1938.

Some authors and illustrators turn their work over to their editors and designers to let them "make the book" look as it will in its final version. However, Ted liked to work alongside them, getting involved in every step of the process. His eye for color and composition was nearly perfect. In fact, he often made his own dummies, or samples of the finished product, by cutting and pasting the words and pictures on each page until they were just right. In those days, this meant really using scissors and glue to put pages together. Some of these dummies of his books still exist in museums.

The reviews of Dr. Seuss's *500 Hats* were even stronger than the ones he'd received for *Mulberry Street*. One reviewer stated it was "a complete tale, not too long, not too short, just right." Of all the reviews he would read during his life, Ted's favorite was written about this book. An old college friend wrote "I do not see what is to prevent him from becoming the Grimm of our times." The name "Dr. Seuss" was unusual enough to be easy to remember—if you knew how to say it. Up to this time, Ted had pronounced "Seuss" in the traditional way, "*soice*," but he found that people remembered it better if it were pronounced differently. He let them "mispronounce" *Seuss* so it rhymed with *Goose*—and it has been pronounced this way ever since.

Ted and Helen had been married for eleven years when *The 500 Hats* hit the bookstore shelves. They decided to dedicate this book to their imaginary child, "Chrysanthemum Pearl, age 89 months, going on 90. The Geisels even added her name (and a few others, including Norval, Thnud, and Wickersham) as they signed their Christmas cards. Helen was unable to have children, but that did not keep her and her husband from enjoying their nieces and nephews or the children who came to have their books autographed. When adults asked him why he had no children of his own, Ted usually replied, "You have 'em, I'll amuse 'em."

Ted was as successful a beginning author as Vanguard Press had ever had. It came as no surprise, then, when a powerhouse publisher tried to get Ted to write books for him instead. Bennett Cerf, publisher of Random House, was well-known in the book business. Ted and he met for lunch one day, and they like each other immediately. By the time lunch was over, Ted had agreed to write his next book for Random House. At first Ted felt guilty for leaving the publishing company that had given him his first chance. Vanguard was a small house, however, and was not able to devote as much time and money to promote Ted's books as he would have liked. He knew that Random House could do this better.

Unfortunately, Ted's first book with Random House was also his first failure as an author. *The Seven Lady Godivas* (1939) was not a children's book. That may have been his first mistake. Adults were not ready (or apparently interested) in buying a book with silly pictures of women and even sillier words about them. Bennett Cerf and Ted knew he was best at writing for children, so they agreed that his next book would bring "the good Dr. Seuss" back to younger readers. His contract with Random House was revised, setting his royalty rates for children's books at 10% for the first 5,000 copies sold and 15% for each copy above 5,000— a very good deal.

Ted shows Helen some sketches. In time the two would share a working relationship with Helen editing Ted's books.

Helen became Ted's best editor, not only on this book, but many more to follow. They worked well together, making sure the words were just right. "Her words are in some of them," Ted said. Ted worked alone on the illustrations. He started by making pencil sketches, side-by-side just as they would appear on facing pages. It usually took him several months before a book was ready to take to his editor. By the end of 1939, Ted's first Random House children's book was published. *The King's Stilts* brought back the character of Bartholomew Cubbins. This story was another fairy tale with Dr. Seuss's strange but wonderful touch. Ted surprised Helen's nieces when he stilt-walked up the front steps of their house on Thanksgiving Day, and continued walking inside the house, then around the dining room table. He told them that he had learned how to walk on stilts when he was doing research for his book.

Ted's next book was born from some doodles. He often sketched random pictures in pencil on tracing paper while trying to think of ideas for new stories. On New Year's Day of 1940 he looked down at a familiar face. The sweet expression that looked back at him belonged to an elephant he'd drawn that seemed related to the blue one that appeared in *Mulberry Street.* Ted left his desk to get a cup of coffee, and when he returned he found that the wind from an open window had blown some of his papers around a bit. Tracing paper is nearly transparent, so something interesting happened when one piece landed on top of another. One paper had the elephant sketch on it; the other had a tree. After the wind did its job, the elephant suddenly looked as if he were sitting high up in a tree. Now *that* was a story! Tree. Elephant. Sitting. Nest. Egg. From this "accidental" event came the next book, *Horton Hatches the Egg.* This was the only book he ever wrote for which he could explain how he had come up with the idea. "I've left a window open by my desk ever since," he once said, "but it never happened again."

He worked hard on this book, as usual, and found he had trouble with two things: what to name the characters and how to get the elephant out of the tree. The main character had many names, such as Osmer, Bosco, and Humphrey, but eventually was named Horton after one of Ted's college friends. The bird was named Bessie, then Saidie, and finally Mayzie. It was up to Helen to help him get Horton back to earth, however. In fact, it was she who wrote the solution: "It's something brand new! IT'S AN ELEPHANT-BIRD!!"

In June 1940, as Ted was in the middle of work on the book, a frightening event took place in Europe. The threat of another world war was in the air. Hitler had taken over the government of Germany and his troops invaded France on June 14. Images of a kind-hearted elephant were pushed aside as Ted began angrily sketching an evil Adolf Hitler instead. More European invasions followed as the summer and fall of 1940 passed. The U.S. had remained neutral militarily but had aided the Allies (France and England) financially. No American soldiers were involved—yet.

Horton Hatches the Egg arrived as fall settled across the country. This book was a remarkable success right away. This book settled any questions Ted had about what he was going to do with his life. He was thirty-six years old. As usual, reviewers adored the Dr. Seuss book. The famous New York toy store, FAO Schwarz, created a big window display featuring an elephant sitting in a tree. Ted enjoyed seeing how people loved his work, and he accepted many invitations at bookstores to do author signings of his books, both for children and adults. He never took his readers lightly. Ted knew it was his job to entertain them with words and pictures. Even so, as

World War II loomed, Ted knew that deadly serious things were happening that he cared about, too. He began drawing political cartoons about the Nazis and Fascists in Europe. Some of these were published in the winter of 1941 in a New York newspaper named *PM*. The editor asked Ted to draw more. For the next seven years, Ted had to turn away from the fantasy world of children's literature to help his country as they faced some very real enemies: Germany and Japan.

Ted and his Irish setter Cluny in La Jolla, California. Ted and Helen moved out to La Jolla and fell in love with the sunny climate.

5

Dr. Seuss Signs Up

IN JUNE OF 1941, Ted and Helen left New York to spend the summer at a house in La Jolla, California. The happy, sun-loving author enjoyed living in California, and he wrote to his editor in New York that he had to "fight rattlesnakes, bees, and man-eating rabbits in the patio." Both he and Helen felt at home in this town near San Diego. Even there, however, the news of Hitler's invasions came through loud and clear. Just as disturbing was the news that the Japanese were becoming hostile, too. Not many Americans were convinced we would be in a war with Japan, but Ted saw it coming.

"Dr. Seuss" put aside his children's books for the next seven years as Ted Geisel turned his talents toward helping our country during a difficult time. Ted was especially upset by Adolf Hitler, who was making his father's homeland an enemy of America. He often drew Hitler as a demanding baby in diapers when doing a political cartoon for *PM* magazine. Later Ted admitted that these cartoons were not his best artwork, but that was because they had to be put together so quickly; he often had to draw as many as five per week.

The Geisels returned to New York in November. Only one month later, as they read the newspaper one Sunday morning, they heard the now-famous radio announcement that the Japanese had bombed Pearl Harbor in Hawaii. It was December 7, 1941—and Ted ran to his drawing board and began drawing furiously. One of his cartoons showed a cat-like Uncle Sam that had been awakened from sleep to find himself at war. On December 8, the U.S. Congress declared war on Japan, and three days later declared war on Germany and Italy.

Suddenly, the U.S. was at war both in Asia against Japan and in Europe against Hitler's Germany. Ted's cartoons drew a lot of attention, both good and bad. People who wanted the U.S. to stay out of the war did not like his cartoons. *Newsweek* magazine, however, said they were "razor-keen." The Treasury Department and the War Production Board also liked his work and commissioned Ted to create posters to help the war effort. By summer 1942, Ted and Helen had returned to California, where he kept busy with posters and cartoons. Living on the west coast was interesting for them. Threats and rumors of Japanese invasions of San Diego made it necessary for the military to practice maneuvers in case such an attack really would take place. The Geisels often saw dive-bombing airplanes, numerous boats, and even some tanks in their area.

Ted was frustrated that he was not able to do more to help the war cause, so he signed up for the navy, requesting to work in naval intelligence. Before he could be accepted, he was offered a commission with the army. He was stationed with the Signal Corps, headed by the Academy-Award-winning movie director Frank Capra, in Hollywood, California. Headquartered at a Fox studio near Sunset Boulevard, this unit was responsible to create film footage for the troops. Some of the nation's best animators and illustrators were there, too. P.D. Eastman, who later illustrated some of Dr. Seuss's Beginner Books, met Ted at "Fort Fox," as they called the place. Well-known animation artists Friz Freleng and Chuck Jones of Warner Brothers were among the talented men of the unit. Colonel Theodor Geisel wore a uniform and practiced drills, just as any soldier would, but his weapon against the enemy was words and pictures, not guns.

Helen moved to Hollywood with Ted and kept busy with her own writing while Ted was at Fox Studios. Helen wrote for Disney and Golden Books, and she preferred to write in prose. In all her attempts to write children's books, only one was rejected. Some of her better-known books include *Three Caballeros, Donald Duck Sees South America,* and *Walt Disney's Surprise Package*, and later Ted said that it was she who supported them financially during the war. She and her husband did not like Los Angeles as well as they enjoyed La Jolla. The city was big, was packed with commuters on the highways, and was starting to be covered by a strange smoke that became known as "smog."

The Fort Fox unit put together newsreels for soldiers to see, creating a new one every two weeks. Part of the newsreel which kept the troops informed of news about the war included cartoons. These cartoons usually had to do with some element of training that the men needed to learn. At first, the film troop used real actors for these pieces, but they soon found that the soldiers responded much better to animated pieces. This was where Ted learned about animated cartoons, something that would be important later in his career. He and Chuck Jones became especially good friends.

Ted's greatest work during the war was not a cartoon, however. After being promoted to major, Ted began work on a special project—a film for soldiers who, at the end of the war, would move into Germany, free it, and bring it back to health. The film, *Your Job in Germany,* had to be reviewed and accepted by the American generals. This meant Ted had to go to Europe, near the fighting itself, to show the film. He would hear bombs streaking over his head and the loud thuds of artillery hitting their mark. At one point, Ted found himself in a frightening place. "We learned we were ten miles behind German lines. We were trapped three days before being rescued by the British," he later explained. Once his mission was finished and the generals approved of his film, Ted returned to California. It was January 1945. Only three months later, Germany would fall to the Allied forces and his film was ready to be used as it was intended. Later, the film was remade as a documentary and won an Academy Award in 1946.

The war ended when the Japanese surrendered in August 1945. Ted and Helen's celebration of peace did not last long, however. On September 14, 1945, Ted's dear sister Marnie died of a heart attack at only forty-three years of age. Her death was one of the few things that Ted could never talk about, as he missed her terribly. Ted and Helen became like parents to Marnie's daughter Peggy, who loved her uncle and aunt and knew they would always be available if she needed them. Helen wondered if Dr. Seuss would return to write children's books. A lot had happened in seven years, and being silly and childlike was not as easy as it once had been.

After the war, Ted tried to work on more films in Hollywood for a while. He and Helen worked together to create a documentary about Japan. Hollywood was a very frustrating experience for Ted, who was used to having more control over the things he made. In the end, after thirty-two revisions, *Design for Death* was shown and gathered strong reviews. In 1947, it won the Academy Award for best documentary feature. But two years later, the film mysteriously disappeared and has not been seen since.

The late 1940s and the 1950s became the era of the "Baby Boomers," a time when family life became more important than ever before. A new area of housing, called the suburbs, emerged as families built homes away from the bustle of the city. Children were born in record numbers, which was good news to the children's book business. The Great Depression was over and the economy grew stronger each year. People had money to spend, and they liked to spend it on their children. The timing was perfect for Dr. Seuss to reappear. By 1946 Ted was no longer satisfied working as a filmmaker, and he knew it was time to renew his relationship with the publishing world—and with Bennett Cerf at Random

House in particular. Ted was pleased to find that many new improvements had come along to make book printing even more visually appealing. These new printing methods allowed many more colors to be used on the page. Nothing could have made Dr. Seuss happier. In short order, Ted made two decisions: first, to return to his work as a children's writer and illustrator, and second, to move to sunny California permanently. He said that he liked the idea of being able "to walk around outside in my pajamas."

The warm climate was the perfect place for Ted to begin his next book, *McElligot's Pool,* published in 1947. Marco, reappearing as a main character, fishes in a pool where he imagines the strangest aquatic creatures ever: a half-cow fish, a kangaroo-like fish, and a dog-fish. Experts praised the illustrations as Seuss's best ever. The watercolors he chose for this book were rich and beautiful, fitting the waterworld he had created. Few people were surprised when *McElligot's Pool* won a Caldecott award. The Caldecott Medal winner and Caldecott Honor books are chosen as the best-illustrated books each year. The book also became a Junior Literary Guild selection, a distinction that set it apart from other picture books. Though it received high honors, this was the only book Ted ever made using watercolors, as he felt that children preferred the brighter colors he had used before.

In 1948 the next Seuss book appeared. Simply offering only red, black, and blue throughout, *Thidwick the Big-Hearted Moose* happily greeted children and adults and became Ted's second Junior Literary Guild selection. Thidwick is a gentle moose who lets others take advantage of his goodness. In the end, however, the freeloaders get what's coming to them and Thidwick is just as

Ted talking to children in La Jolla, California. Ted and Helen decided to move to La Jolla for good in 1948.

big-hearted as ever. According to one reviewer, "this is also what the child expects." This was also the year that Ted and Helen finally moved to La Jolla, California to a place they called The Tower because it actually was a tower on Mount Soledad, high above the rest of the town. Ted and Helen made this their home for the rest of their lives.

On a literary roll, Ted continued to create a book a year. He loved his new workroom, overlooking the Pacific Ocean and the beautiful southern California coastline. But when it was time to work, Ted turned his back to the beauty so it would not distract him. He set himself an eight-hour schedule, seven days a week. Sometimes he worked much longer, late into the night, taking only short breaks. He still used the same wooden drawing board that he had started with in New York during the 1930s. All around were containers holding colored pencils, stained paint brushes, and stubs of erasers. Ted seldom threw away anything on his desk, including one-inch long pencils that had been used as much as they could be.

Typically Ted sat in a high-backed chair, swiveling back and forth as he thought. He first drew his illustrations on tracing paper, then would draw the pictures and write the words for one page, perfecting it before starting on the next. This often took draft after draft before he was ready to draw his final illustration on heavy paper with a felt-tip pen. His pile of throw-away drafts was called "the bone pile." If he got stuck in his writing, Ted often paced back and forth across the room—or, if he was really "blocked," he would pick out one of his many hats and wear it until an idea came to him. "It's hard," he once said. "I'm a bleeder and I sweat at it . . . You have to remember that in a children's book a paragraph is like a chapter in an adult book, and a sentence is like a paragraph." Other times, Ted would lie on a couch in his workroom and read a mystery novel until he was a little tired. He said his "best stuff" was written when he was "a bit tired."

Some of his ideas came more easily than others,

though. Resurrecting Marco had been a good idea in *McElligot's Pool,* Ted figured, so why not bring back Bartholomew Cubbins, the boy with 500 hats? In 1949, *Bartholomew and the Oobleck* gave children the goo of their dreams: gloppy green goo called "oobleck" that rains over everything in the kingdom. "I didn't dream it up," Ted said about the idea. While in Europe during World War II, he overheard a soggy soldier complain, "Rain, always rain! Why can't we have something different for a change?" That was all Ted needed to get his creative wheels turning. In the story, the King gets his magicians to change the rain, snow, and fog to

Did you know...

After his long time-out from creating children's books in the 1940s, Ted Geisel jumped back in with some old ideas—and some new ones, too. His next book, *McElligot's Pool,* had the same character (Marco) and a similar pace and rhythm as *Mulberry Street.* The illustrations were different, however. As the action builds, the movement of Marco and the Seussian fishes moves dramatically to the right, drawing the reader to turn page after page. For the first time, Ted used watercolors. The colors were so unusual and varied that the publishing company said it would cost too much to print it that way. Not one to let that stop him, Ted offered a compromise. Every other two-page spread is completely black-and-white. It cut the color costs in half and Ted kept his watercolors where he most wanted them.

oobleck. Disaster results when everything is smothered by the goo. Then, like verbal magic, the goo stops falling only after the great king admits, "It's all my fault." Ted won his second Caldecott Honor Award for this gooey tale, which has only two colors: black and (of course) green.

Ted overcame his stage fright temporarily when he was asked to speak at a writer's conference in 1949. The trick he used when the fear started to rise up inside him was to find a chalkboard and sketch illustrations all over it. His panic nearly returned when he discovered all of his drawings had been erased by a janitor who thought "some kids really messed up the blackboard." Ted pushed through, however, and offered some simple advice to the would-be authors who came to learn from him. "Write a verse a day," he told them, "not to send to publishers, but to throw in waste baskets. It will help your prose . . . Shorten paragraphs and sentences, then shorten words . . . Use verbs. Let the kids fill in the adjectives." After the conference ended, Ted thought it was important for him to start work in a book about children's book writing. His editor did not feel as strongly as Ted. He preferred that Dr. Seuss return to writing his own books rather than telling others how to do it. Although quite disappointed by the rejection of his idea, Ted began work on his next project, *If I Ran the Zoo*.

While settling into his new home in California, Ted often thought back about his childhood in Springfield on Fairfield Street. Some of the most vivid memories included the sights, sounds, smells, and impressions of the Springfield Zoo where he, his father, and his sister had spent time exploring the animal kingdom. More and more, his thoughts ran wild about the zoo. Staring out his window, Ted began an imaginative journey that would become one of his funniest, warmest books ever. *If I Ran the Zoo* appeared in 1950 to glowing reviews and eventually another Caldecott Honor Award. A new decade was underway, and Dr. Seuss was just getting warmed up.

Ted holds up a copy of The Cat In The Hat. *Published in 1957, it was written using only 225 specific words that his editor had picked out for him as a challenge.*

New Dreams—and One Bad Nightmare

WITH EIGHT SUCCESSFUL children's books already claiming space in bookstores all across the country, Dr. Seuss still found himself thinking about making films in Hollywood. He stayed in touch with some of his World War II buddies who continued to work there. One in particular, P.D. Eastman, was an illustrator with the new United Productions of America studio. While most studios were using the same kinds of storylines in their cartoons, UPA wanted to try something different. Eastman knew that Ted Geisel was just the person to approach. No one had proven to have fresher ideas than

Dr. Seuss. And, as usual, Ted did not disappoint his friend or his fans.

Seuss's first full-length children's cartoon started from one big idea: "Just suppose," said Dr. Seuss, "there was a little kid who didn't speak words but only weird sounds?" For his new story, Ted was paid five hundred dollars. Because he felt he was not good at drawing people, Ted wanted someone else to do the illustrations for the cartoon. *Gerald McBoing McBoing* was about a "different" kid who is teased and pushed aside because he makes strange noises, like a horse's neigh or a squeaky door. After running away, Gerald is "discovered" by a man who wants the boy to make his noises as special effects on the radio. His talent is finally recognized, and Gerald is a big success—and after the film was seen by thousands of people, Ted and UPA Studios were successful as well. *Gerald McBoing McBoing* won an Academy Award in 1951 for best cartoon. At the same time, copies of *If I Ran the Zoo* were selling as fast as they hit the shelves. Was there anything Ted could fail at doing?

Helen had worked tirelessly with Ted as his editor and critic and as his assistant in answering his mail and phone calls. In responding to some of the fan letters, she even signed herself as "Mrs. Dr. Seuss." But the pace was difficult for Helen, and her health was affected. She was tired and suffered from painful ulcers, but kept working, happy for Ted's success. And things were just beginning to get even busier.

The thrill of working with film was alive in Ted again. He sent an idea for another feature-length film to Columbia Studios. The three-time Academy Award winner was offered a $35,000 advance for his newest idea, a fantasy film called *The 5,000 Fingers of Dr. T.* This time, he planned to include real children in the movie, not only animated characters. The plot centered around one boy who hated taking piano lessons and his rescue of hundreds of other children who were enslaved to their pianos by the evil Dr. Terwilliger. Happy beyond description, Ted expected to become immersed in the film process and to have control over "his" project. Helen, however, was concerned that this might be one of the busiest years of their lives— and a year without a new book. She knew that this was one of Ted's greatest dreams, and she was willing to sacrifice whatever was needed to make him happy. In fact, the Geisels rented an apartment in Los Angeles so Ted could easily get to the studio each weekday. On the weekends, Ted and Helen returned to La Jolla.

What began as a grand idea and thrilling experience quickly dissolved into trouble. Ted wrote the screenplay and the lyrics to the songs, but someone or other was constantly changing things. The changes continued to happen, causing the production of the film to be postponed three times. Only his set designs stayed true to the Seuss style. At one point, Ted told the producer that he was leaving the film because the script changes were more than he could tolerate. Some compromising took place, and Ted stayed on. A year after beginning the project, the cast was finally ready for filming, but suddenly a need for budget cuts was announced. For example, where the script had once called for 500 boy pianists (from which the title *5,000 Fingers* comes), only 150 were really used. Ted recalls one day on the set that actually became a happy memory for him. One day, someone made the mistake of paying each of the boys his weekly pay rather than giving it to the child's parent or agent. After a hotdog spending spree at the lunchroom, one of the boys threw up all over his piano. "This started a chain reaction, causing one after another of the boys to go queasy in the greatest mass upchuck in the history of Hollywood," said Ted. He added, "When the picture was finally released, the critics reacted in much the same manner." When the film was previewed, most of the audience left the theater after only fifteen minutes. For the rest of his life, Ted described making this film as "the worst experience of my life." He even refused to list it in his biography at Random House.

After the filming was finished, Ted hurried back to his office in La Jolla to finish his next book for Random House, one that had been due in January. In May, Ted was still at work on *Scrambled Eggs Super!* He had missed the chance to have it available to bookstores by Christmas. It came out in March 1953, just before Ted and Helen sailed for Japan. *Life* magazine had asked Ted to write a piece for them about the children of Japan. On board ship, the Geisels studied information about how Japan had changed since World War II. His job was to find out how the war had changed the hopes and plans of the children there.

Ted crossed the language barrier by having the children do what he best understood: drawing. He asked them to draw pictures of what they wanted to be when they grew up. In all, he collected more than 15,000 drawings. Not surprisingly, the drawings often reflected a more modern kind of thinking—and more Americanized thinking, too. Boys saw themselves being pilots and girls wanted to be hostesses, much like flight attendants. Though Ted adored children and the work he accomplished in Japan, he was disappointed once again when the editors of *Life* changed his article to reflect their own ideas instead of Ted's view. Even so, his and Helen's adventures in Japan helped soothe the irritation of the *5,000 Fingers* fiasco.

He was determined to let go of the film world and to fully embrace his greatest gift: writing and illustrating children's book. But could he make a real living doing only that? After all, he was earning only a few hundred dollars a year from royalties. Most of his other work, mainly in advertising and filmmaking, had kept him financially secure. Fortunately, the Baby Boom would make it possible for Dr. Seuss to earn more than enough.

Ted and Helen settled in as citizens of La Jolla, even joining some civic groups so they could get involved in the community. The Geisels made many friends and loved to socialize. Ted was especially fond of playing practical jokes, as always, and Helen often had to talk him out of his most ridiculous ideas. When things were not going well with his writing, Ted would walk around his property, looking at the plants and moving rocks here and there, arranging them in ways that pleased him. Ted's best loved "rock" was carefully placed in a shaded garden. Many years previously, Ted's father had given him a rock that held a true dinosaur's footprint. Over the years, Ted had taken that rock with him whenever he moved. Finally, it found a permanent home.

In late 1953, Ted started a new book using his beloved character Horton the elephant. Written in verse (this one actually has the same rhythm as "Twas the Night Before Christmas"), Ted used his experience in Japan to develop a wonderful theme: "A person's a person no matter how small." *Horton Hears a Who* was very much a joint effort between Ted and Helen. She helped him maintain his rhythm while not losing sight of the message. In early 1954, the Geisels went to New York to hand-deliver the manuscript and illustrations. The editors and publisher gathered in one office as Ted read the story aloud, and there was no

Ted holds the head of one of his characters, a blue-green abelard. Creating strange and fantastical creatures had been a Geisel theme since the start of his cartooning career

doubt that another Seuss best-seller had just been born.

Traveling, writing, speaking, and entertaining kept Ted and Helen under pressure throughout 1954. This year brought many challenges, and one great honor. Ted was called to receive an honorary doctorate degree from his college, Dartmouth. The Geisels were excited, but decided to keep the news to themselves for a while. During a party to celebrate the new concert season in La Jolla, someone mentioned a new article in *Life* magazine that suggested Dr. Seuss might be a good author/illustrator to take on the job of making reading fun for school children. The *Dick and Jane* reading books all the children were using lacked imagination and style. Ted might have become immersed in this project right away if Helen's health had not suddenly taken a turn for the worse. Within twenty-four hours of the party, Helen was in great pain and quickly became paralyzed from the neck down.

Doctors at first were puzzled by her symptoms, but they diagnosed her with Guillain-Barré Syndrome, a typically fatal disease. Because Helen could not breathe on her own, she was placed in a machine called an iron lung, which would breathe for her. This is a large metal machine in which a patient's entire body is placed. Only her head stuck out, and a mirror was placed above her. The doctors told Ted that her chance of surviving was very small.

Helen's condition worsened over the next two weeks, to the point that she did not recognize Ted any longer. Ted stayed near her, and at night helped the nurses by carrying things for them. He called Dartmouth College to tell them he would not be able to attend the ceremony to receive his degree. Each day that Helen survived was "a miracle." Ted's devotion to her was strong, and somehow Helen began to fight back. Soon she was able to breathe on her own and she could swallow again. Ted brought her Popsicles to help her practice swallowing. In July, she no longer needed the iron lung at all. Transferred to a rehabilitation hospital that month, Helen started her long journey back. Eventually she would regain the abilities to talk and walk again. She had to learn the most basic things, such as buttoning a button or combing her hair, all over again. Ted took an apartment near the hospital so he could take care of the business and do some work. This was not easy for him, because Helen had always taken care of everything. He had not kept a checkbook or even made coffee in decades—but somehow he managed.

In August, Helen was well enough to enjoy Ted's happy news that *Horton Hears a Who* was receiving positive reviews. In September she was able to move back to La Jolla, but she could not be left alone. Despite the pain and difficulty, Helen worked hard at her physical therapy and made good progress. Through it all, Helen described Ted as "part man, part angel." Now that Helen was recovering, a very relieved and happy Ted had renewed energy to work on new projects, including his next book *On Beyond Zebra* (1955), which took children beyond the letter *Z* into such new ones as Yuzz and Vroo. Ted dedicated this book to Helen.

A few months later in June of 1956, Ted finally accepted his honorary doctorate degree from Dartmouth, making him "Dr. Dr. Seuss," as he liked to joke. Robert Frost, a great American poet, was also honored that year, and Ted said later that "I very carefully refrained from mentioning the kind of poetry I write." The same year, Ted's twelfth children's book was published. Modeled after the popular *If I Ran the Zoo,* Ted wrote *If I Ran the Circus* and dedicated it to his father. Ted's next book, however, would change reading for children all over the country and would make Dr. Seuss one of the most recognized children's authors in the United States.

Previously, in 1955, Ted had traveled to Boston to meet with the head of publishing at Houghton Mifflin's education division. William Spaulding was concerned about the research that showed American children were becoming weaker readers. He felt that classroom teachers needed to have better reading books to share with their students that had great illustrations as well as good stories. Dr. Seuss, Spaulding believed, was just the one to help out. During their meeting, he told Ted, "Write me a story that first-graders can't put down!" Then he handed Ted a list of 225 words, challenging him to use only those words when he wrote the new book. Ted was interested in the concept, but first had to complete work on *If I Ran the Circus*. Because of Ted's contract with Random House, the publisher at Houghton Mifflin would have to get Cerf Bennett, Ted's publisher, to agree. In the end, Houghton Mifflin was allowed to sell a school edition to schools only, and Random House sold their trade edition in bookstores as usual.

The limitations of a word list made writing more difficult than Ted had expected, but it helped to have his main character clearly in mind—a mischievous cat who gets two children caught up in some craziness. No other character is as widely recognized as Dr. Seuss's Cat in the Hat, costumed in a tall red and white striped hat and a red bow tie with three—instead of the usual two— loops. It is interesting to note that Ted often sketched cats, though he preferred dogs as pets. (Unfortunately, he never learned to draw dogs.) *The Cat in the Hat* appeared in 1957. One critic said it was "the most influential

Did you know...

Ted struggled and struggled to write his thirteenth children's book. As he looked at the list of 225 words William Spaulding of Houghton Mifflin had given him, Ted cried out to his wife Helen, "There are no adjectives!" He decided he would start by making a title from the first two words that rhymed on the list. Those two words were *cat* and *hat*. *The Cat in the Hat* had a title, but the story took a year to complete. Sometimes Ted would get so frustrated by the limitations of the word list that he would throw the manuscript across the room. But all his efforts were rewarded—in its first three years, almost 100 million copies of *The Cat in the Hat* were sold, with translations in Braille, French, Chinese, and Swedish. Ted never again had to worry about earning a living from his books.

first-grader since McGuffey." The McGuffey Readers had been used to teach reading for well over 100 years.

Schools were slower to catch on than the general public. Ted explained, "Parents understood better than school people the necessity for this kind of reader." In the beginning, bookstore sales of *The Cat in the Hat* (cover price, $1.95) exceeded 12,000 a month. The success of this new kind of book gave Cerf Bennett's wife Phyllis an idea. Why not set up a Random House division just for this kind of reader? She asked Ted to consider writing four or five more of these beginner books right away, promising that they would not be sold or marketed to compete with his "big books," which did not have the same restrictions as the beginner books. In the spring of 1957, Beginner Books was launched, with Ted as the president of the division and Helen Geisel as a third partner. This was Ted's chance to work with new writers and develop a much-needed reading resource for children. Soon a needlepoint picture of the Cat was hung at the Geisels' house. It read "This cat started a publishing house. No other cat can make this claim."

Even as he was starting the new publishing company, Ted was in the middle of his next "big book." While *The Cat in the Hat* was the hardest book he had written thus far, *How the Grinch Stole Christmas* was the easiest. Seuss's main character was a villain, a creature with a heart "two sizes too small." Ted was 53 years old in 1957, so it seems no accident that this bad guy had hated Christmas for 53 years. Ever since, the word "grinch" has stood for a person who is mean-spirited and wants to spoil other people's fun. Ted must have loved the name, because he had the license plates for his Cadillac changed to spell "GRINCH." The story exposed the greediness of a commercialized Christmas season. In the end, the moral is summed up by the Grinch himself as he says, "Maybe Christmas doesn't come from a store. Maybe Christmas . . . means a little bit more!" Not surprisingly, Ted was careful about the neverending requests to use his characters on children's novelty items, such as lunch boxes, coloring books, and toys. He rarely agreed to this kind of business arrangement for fear it would cheapen what he was working hard to create.

Meanwhile, as sales of *Grinch* multiplied, Ted got busy with the new enterprise. Phyllis Bennett had created "the" word list, made up of 379 words from which the

THE GRINCH

A drawing of the Grinch, one of Dr. Seuss' most enduring characters from his Christmas book How The Grinch Stole Christmas.

writer could use up to 220. Dr. Seuss's next Beginner Book was a sequel to his first. *The Cat in the Hat Comes Back* met a waiting public in 1958. Later that year, the next in the series arrived, too—*Yertle the Turtle and*

Other Stories. Also that year, Ted received the Lewis Carroll literary award from the University of Wisconsin. Four more Beginner Books were already underway by other writers and illustrators, including *A Fly Went By* by Mike McClintock, the eager editor who had given Ted his start in 1937. The Cat from *The Cat in the Hat* became the official logo for the entire series, and Ted was finally the success he had always hoped to be.

Ted holding a sketch entitled "Cat Carnival in West Venice—Probably in Italy." Although he preferred dogs to cats in real life, he had never learned to draw dogs!

7

Busy, Busy Dr. Seuss

THE FIVE SEUSS books that tickled his readers in 1957 and 1959 were just the beginning of what would be the most productive time in Ted Geisel's life. *Happy Birthday to You*, published in 1959, was for anyone who had a birthday—and that was everyone! Critics, as usual, let the world know that dear Dr. Seuss had delivered another wonderful, silly book. While this "big book" keeping booksellers and librarians busy, Ted was well underway with his next Beginner Book, *One Fish Two Fish Red Fish Blue Fish,* one of the longest titles of a Dr. Seuss book. Again limited by the 220-word list,

Ted focused on colors and creatures as he rhymed his way along, delighting readers with fun sounds and bright colors. In fact, when Ted took his final draft to Random House, he showed up with three crayon pieces to show his editors exactly which three colors he wanted in his book: bright yellow, deep red, and an amazing turquoise. The crayon stubs remained the standard, until Ted was content that the inks matched exactly. Then he and Helen took a much-deserved vacation.

Beginner Books was an immediate success. By early 1960, the division had sales of more than one million dollars. Eighteen different Beginner Books were already available, and plans for many more were already underway. Ready for another challenge, Ted took a fifty-dollar bet from his friend and publisher Cerf Bennett that he could not write a Beginner Book using only 50 words. *Green Eggs and Ham,* Ted admitted, "was the only book I ever wrote that still makes me laugh." Slated for sale in fall 1960, *Green Eggs and Ham* was ready in April for the editors to review. After reading the manuscript aloud to the staff at Random House (including Cerf Bennett), everyone knew Ted had done it again, and he won the bet easily. By the end of the year, five of the country's top sixteen best-selling children's books were written and illustrated by Dr. Seuss.

Ted had already written some stories with a political or social theme, such as *Horton Hears a Who* and *Yertle the Turtle.* His next book, *The Sneetches and Other Stories* (1960), was a Seuss "big book" that clearly spoke to the issue of racism. Some Sneetches had stars on their bellies; some did not. The starred group felt superior to the other, and there was no getting along between them. In the end, their prejudices were shown for what they were—ridiculous—and both groups learned to live happily together.

Helen had also been busy writing books, most of them for Beginning Books under her maiden name, Helen Palmer. Her book *A Fish Out of Water* was published in 1961. That fall, she and Ted traveled to England, where they discovered that Dr. Seuss was not nearly as popular as he was in the U.S. In fact, more of his books were sold for adult reading than for children, and prisoners were even taught to read using them.

In 1962, marking the 25th anniversary of Ted's first book, Random House published another "big book,"

Did you know...

Ted Geisel used exactly 50 different words in *Green Eggs and Ham*. To keep track of this, Ted made huge charts and lists as he worked on the story. Only one word in the entire book had more than one syllable—*anywhere*—and he used it only eight times. Most people felt that what made this book so much fun was how Ted turned phrases inside-out. "Ham and eggs" became "eggs and ham," and "I am Sam" became "Sam-I-am." Dr. Seuss's *Green Eggs and Ham*, in addition to becoming one of the the best-selling, most beloved Seuss book of all time, also changed Ted's diet. For the rest of his life, Dr. Seuss was served green eggs and ham wherever he went. The music group Moxy Früvous turned the Seuss rhyme into a rap song, and Rev. Jesse Jackson read it as a sermon on *Saturday Night Live*.

Dr. Seuss's Sleep Book. The next year, 1963, Dr. Seuss helped new readers by providing them with two new Beginner Books: *Hop on Pop* and *Dr. Seuss's ABC Book.* Beginner Books were tagged as "The Simplest Seuss for Youngest Use." Ted was receiving about 2,000 fan letters a week, many of them from children telling Dr. Seuss how much they liked his rhymes. A nine-year-old child wrote about one of his books, "It's the funniest book I ever read in nine years."

Ted and Helen traveled to one of their favorite countries in 1964. Australia was a magical place for Ted and he told people he would move there if he were twenty years younger. Helen enjoyed the trip, too, but returned to California very tired. She had not fully recovered from the Guillain-Barré Syndrome, and seemed to become more disabled as each year passed. Still, she continued to write, and received good reviews for her next Beginner Book, *Do You Know What I'm Going to Do Next Saturday?*, which was published in 1963.

Ted's next Beginner Book was a book of tongue twisters called *Fox in Socks.* It had a fun "warning" on the cover, which read:

> This is a book you READ ALOUD to find out just how smart your tongue is. The first time you read it, don't go fast! This Fox is a tricky fox. He'll try to get your tongue in trouble.

Even as he was writing both the "big books" (his next one was *I Had Trouble in Getting to Solla Sollew* in 1965) and the Beginner Books as Dr. Seuss, Ted was also writing books under his old pseudonym, Theo LeSeig. These Beginner Books were written by Ted but illustrated by others. These included *Ten Apples Up on*

Top (1961), *I Wish I Had Duck Feet* (1965), and *Come on Over to My House* (1966).

In 1966, Chuck Jones, one of Ted's old friends from the war films, told Ted that he wanted to make a television show using one of Dr. Seuss's books. Television in the '60s was the newest, best source of entertainment because almost every family owned a TV, and color TV was becoming more affordable as well. Still unhappy with the failure from *The 5,000 Fingers of Dr. T,* Ted was not interested. Helen encouraged Ted to think about Chuck's request, and with her guidance, Ted listened to his friend and embarked upon this labor of love. Finally in Christmas 1966, *How the Grinch Stole Christmas* glowed from televisions in living rooms everywhere, becoming one of America's most beloved television programs ever. (It would become a major motion picture starring Jim Carrey in 2000.) Ted especially loved writing the new parts of the story, in particular the lyrics to "The Grinch Song," that describe the Grinch: "You're cuddly as a cactus, you're as charming as an eel." The biggest challenge in making the show was to stretch a twelve-minute story (as it was read from the book) into a thirty-minute program. The show was the most expensive half-hour TV program made up to that time, and it was shown on December 18, 1966 at 7:00 p.m. As a result of the television version, adults and children renewed their love of Seussian tales and bought his books in record-breaking numbers.

Encouraged by the success of *Grinch,* Ted agreed to the production of *Horton Hears a Who!* as a 1967 Thanksgiving children's television special. Sadly, Helen did not live to see it as she passed away on October 23, 1967, at the age of 69. Ted struggled to get on with his

A scene from the animated adapation of How The Grinch Stole Christmas. *Although Ted was reluctant to do another movie adaptation following the debacle of* The 5000 Fingers of Dr. T, *his animator friend Chuck Jones and Helen convinced him to do it, and the program is now an enduring Christmas television classic.*

work. Helen had been his wife, his friend, his editor, and his best helper for more than forty years. He had to complete a new kind of book for Beginner Books, one aimed at even younger readers. Bright & Early Books were meant for "pre-readers," or children who were just starting to look at books. The first one of its kind was Dr. Seuss's *The Foot Book*, which was published in 1968. Repetition and rhyme made each page easy to remember, and therefore easy to read. Ted's talent sprang to life as he wrote lines like "Left foot/Left foot/Right foot/Right/Feet in the morning/Feet at night." Clearly, the need to create new books helped Ted through the grief of losing Helen.

A year after Helen's death, Ted married a long-time friend of his and Helen's, Audrey Stone. She helped Ted renew his love of travel, and they spent much of 1969 going from Hawaii, to Japan, to Cambodia, to India, to Israel, to Paris, to London, and finally back to New York. In Japan, Ted was glad to celebrate the new Japanese edition of *The Cat in the Hat.* The newly-weds returned to New York just in time for the release of Ted's newest "big book," *I Can Lick 30 Tigers Today! and Other Stories*, which was dedicated to Audrey. That same year, a Theo LeSeig Beginner Book, *My Book About Me*, also was published. After Ted and Audrey returned to the Geisel home in La Jolla, California, the good Dr. Seuss got back to work right away. Two Seuss books came out in 1970: *I Can Draw It Myself by Me, Myself* (a "big book") and *Mr. Brown Can Moo! Can You?* (a Beginner Book). Ted called the first one "a revolt against coloring books." He followed it with *I Can Write—by Me, Myself* in 1971.

Ted's interest in social and political issues was renewed,

too. Over several years, he had watched the beautiful California skies grow grayer and thicker, and the land had become cluttered with too many buildings. The sadness of seeing the scenery change so much and seeing people disinterested in preserving nature made Ted yearn to travel again. He and Audrey headed for Kenya in September 1970. At the Mt. Kenya Safari Club, Ted watched the African wildlife literally walk past him. One day he saw a herd of elephants walk by and suddenly Ted was energized with ideas. In one afternoon, he wrote most of his next book which became *The Lorax*. The scenery in that book resembles the terrain of the Serengheti of Kenya. The book addressed the environmental issues of conservation and pollution. In 1971, a book like this was unusual, and some critics did not know what to make of such a serious Seuss. First Lady Ladybird Johnson loved it, however, and asked Ted to donate the original art and manuscript to the Lyndon B. Johnson Presidential Library in Austin, Texas. Ted later said that this "really makes me feel sort of good." Few people would be surprised to know that *The Lorax* was Ted's favorite book of all. The next year, *The Lorax* made its appearance as a television special, for which Ted won an award at the International Animated Cartoon Festival in Europe. He had already won the coveted Peabody Award for both *The Grinch* and *Horton Hears a Who!* in 1971.

Ted continued to work closely with other writers and illustrators at Beginner Books, including Stan and Jan Berenstain (authors of the *Berenstain Bears* series) and Richard Scarry. A new pseudonym of Ted's was born in the 1970s too. Rosetta Stone (named partly for Audrey) became the pen name on the books that Ted cowrote with Mike Frith, a Beginner Books editor. Over the next several years, a very happy Ted Geisel turned out book after book: *Marvin K. Mooney Will You Please Go Now!* (Bright & Early Books, 1972), *In a People House* (as Theo LeSeig, 1972), *The Many Mice of Mr. Brice* (as Theo LeSeig, 1973), *Did I Ever Tell You How Lucky You Are?* ("big book," 1973), *The Shape of Me and Other Stuff* (Bright & Early Books, 1973), *Wacky Wednesday* (as Theo LeSeig, 1974), *A Great Day for Up!* (as Theo LeSeig, 1974), *There's a Wocket in My Pocket!* (as Theo LeSeig, 1974), *Because a Little Bug Went Ka-Choo!* (as Rosetta Stone, 1975), *Oh, The Thinks You Can Think!* (Beginner Books, 1975), and *Would You Rather Be a Bullfrog?* (as Theo LeSeig, 1975).

In 1974, a popular newspaper columnist named Art Buchwald used one of Dr. Seuss's books to make a political statement. He changed only the name in *Marvin K. Mooney*, and made history. On July 30, 1974, Buchwald printed in his column:

> Richard M. Nixon, will you please go now!
> The time has come.
> The time is now.
> Just go.
> Go.
> Go! . . .

About a week later, President Richard M. Nixon resigned after months of scandal associated with his administration. Both Art Buchwald and his new friend Ted Geisel rejoiced.

Unfortunately, Ted's hard work, late hours, and heavy smoking began to catch up with him. His first wife, Helen, had tried unsuccessfully for years to get Ted to quit smoking and to get more rest. One morning in 1975, Ted shouted at Audrey, "Am I going blind? I can't focus!

Everything is squiggly." His eyesight had been deteriorating over the past few years, and cataracts was to blame. Ted worked through it by remembering what a certain color "felt" like as he reached for a crayon with a certain nick in it. Now he had also developed glaucoma, a more serious disease. Over the next five years, Ted endured several surgeries and treatments. Nothing terrified Ted more as an illustrator than the prospect that he might go blind. As he continued to work on books, Ted improvised by making his illustrations extra-large, easier for him to see. It was difficult for Ted to see himself in the mirror, so he decided to grow a beard so he wouldn't have to shave. He followed his doctors' orders and thankfully, Ted's sight improved. In those years, he still wrote and drew with as much talent as ever, finishing *The Cat's Quizzer*, a Beginner Book, for publication in 1976. Then he wrote *I Can Read with My Eyes Shut!* (Beginner Books, 1978) as a tribute to his vision ordeal. He dedicated the book to one of his doctors, "David Worthen, E. G.* (*Eye Guy)." He also finished two books as Theo LeSeig between 1974 and 1978: *Hooper Humperdink. . .? Not Him!* (1975) and *Try to Remember the First of Octember* (1977).

In 1979, Theodor Seuss Geisel turned 75. He especially liked the gold cufflinks of the Cat in the Hat he received from a friend, but otherwise was not too excited about turning 75. He told a reporter, "I meet old, old people, who can scarcely walk, and they say, 'I was brought up on your books.'" Ever young at heart, Ted offered his readers another tongue twister title in the same year, *Oh, Say Can You Say?* Readers also enjoyed his newest Theo LeSeig book, *The Hair Book.* In 1980, Ted received the Laura Ingalls Wilder Award for his "lasting contributions to children's literature."

The previous five years had been productive, despite the problems with his vision. He had to wear an eye patch for a time. He wrote, telling someone, "For the next several weeks, I'll continue to have double vision, which causes me to burp and bite people and dogs." When the patch was removed, Ted's vision was completely restored. At 76, Dr. Seuss was at his prime.

Ted shakes hands with the Cat In The Hat.

8

"We Can Do Better Than This"

WITH HIS EYESIGHT back to normal, Ted began 1981 with the excitement of a child starting something new. His amazing sense of color was as keen as ever, and he helped staff members at Beginner Books to put the right colors together for new projects. By summer, he was busy at work on his next Random house "big book," *Hunches in Bunches*. He hadn't produced a big book since 1973, partly because of his vision trouble and partly because of his activities with Beginner Books. He was ready to get back to the books he loved best.

In September, as he was putting the final touches on *Hunches in Bunches*, Ted asked for some medicine to ease a case of indigestion. Three days later, he still felt the burning in his chest. Audrey called 911 and Ted was admitted to intensive care. He had suffered a minor heart attack. The doctor told Ted he had to change only one thing about his life: He would have to quit smoking. Helen and Audrey each had done what she could to urge him to quit, but he refused. One evening at a dinner party, Ted even set a small "No Smoking" sign on fire as a message to his hostess. Now he had no choice, as his life was in danger. Not one to do anything like other people, Ted replaced his cigarettes with a pipe. This pipe, however, did not contain tobacco, but was instead filled with some peat moss and a few radish seeds. Every time he wanted to smoke, he simply put the pipe in his mouth, pulled out an eyedropper filled with water, and "watered the radishes." Finishing *Hunches in Bunches* was helpful, though, because it kept Ted's attention on work and not on smoking. Ironically, the book begins, "Do you ever sit and fidget/when you don't know what to do?" Ted knew exactly what that felt like.

Hunches in Bunches came out in the fall of 1982. That season, Ted met another popular children's book author and illustrator, Maurice Sendak, creator of *Where the Wild Things Are.* The two men formed an immediate friendship. Usually Ted was not aware of other children's writers because he was so busy with his own work. He knew Sendak's books, however, and said that if he were a child, those were the books he would read. These authors/ illustrators met with a group of fans in San Diego, where they were asked if they liked their characters. Ted answered, "If my characters gave me a dinner party, I wouldn't show up." Similarly, Sendak responded, "If we lived with them, we'd be in the madhouse." Later Sendak was asked about the real Dr. Seuss. "The Ted Geisel I knew was that rare amalgamation of genial gent and tomcat—a creature content with himself as animal and artist, and one who didn't give a lick or a spit for anyone's opinion, one way or another, of his work . . . Dr. Seuss was serious about not being serious."

In 1983, Ted was thinking about signing a $10 million contract with the Coleco company, a toy manufacturer. This successful company had created the phenomenal Cabbage Patch Kids dolls, and Coleco's marketing leaders wanted to get Seuss's characters in the marketplace, too. Ted and the Coleco people set a date to do the official signing, but other events interrupted. During a regular dental exam, Ted's dentist noticed a suspicious spot at the base of Ted's tongue. A biopsy showed that it was a kind of cancer that smokers sometimes got. Some doctors told Ted that he would have to have a part of his tongue removed in order to save his life. Ted was upset that his speech would be forever affected, so he went elsewhere for a second opinion. Oncologists, or cancer specialists, at the University of California at San Francisco recommended that Ted have two procedures: radiation to the area where the tumor was and an implant that would continue delivering low-dosage radiation to the area afterward. The first procedure would affect his voice. He told the doctors to go ahead with the implant, but that he would not agree to the radiation, even though he knew that the implant alone might not destroy the cancer completely. Two weeks later, after the implant, Ted returned with Audrey to La Jolla.

Ted had seldom been ill, so he was frustrated that his body was interfering with his work. He had a new passion burning in his mind and a book was already "cooking" in his imagination. Not since *The Lorax* had Ted written a book with a political theme. In the 1970s and 1980s the United States and the former Soviet Union were competing with each other to

Dr. Seuss signs a copy of **The Butter Battle Book** *at a party celebrating his* **80th birthday in 1984.** *The Butter Battle Book was written in response to the escalating arms race between the US and the Soviet Union.*

create bigger and more effective nuclear weapons, just in case the other would attack. This "arms race" scared people. Large areas of the planet could be destroyed within minutes if these weapons were ever released. Ted, too, was concerned, and he had something to say about it. Respected as Ted's "most important book Dr. Seuss has ever created" by the people at Random House, *The Butter Battle Book* was unique for Ted because the words all came first, not the drawings. The book came out on Ted's eightieth birthday in 1984 to mixed reviews—some people thought the subject was too much for children while others thought it was the right time to address the issue. *The Butter Battle Book* appeared on *The New York Times* best-seller list for six months—but on the adult list. The book's open ending kept discussions going:

> "Grandpa!" I shouted. "Be careful! Oh, gee!
> Who's going to drop it?
> Will *you* . . . ? Or will *he* . . . ?"
> "Be patient," said Grandpa. "We'll see.
> We will see . . ."

Regardless of people's opinions about this book, Ted won a special Pulitzer Prize in 1984 for his lifetime of

Did you know...

As soon as Ted Geisel finished *the Butter Battle Book,* he said, "I have no idea if this is an adult book for children or a children's book for adults." The serious subject of nuclear war made many people at Random House nervous, and they had their own mini-war about what to do with the book. Some wanted to change the title to *The Yook and the Zooks.* Some wanted a different cover from the cheerleader image Ted had given them. In the end, all of Ted's original ideas won. *The Butter Battle Book* was strongly endorsed by another great author/illustrator, Maurice Sendak. Later, in 1990, the book was made into an animated television special. "Right after that," Ted said proudly, "the U.S.S.R. began falling apart." New York's mayor Ed Koch wrote to Ted that it was "a far, far butter thing you've done" than even his earlier books.

contributions to children's literature. He and Audrey were invited to the White House to meet President and Mrs. Ronald Reagan. Ted could not resist whispering to Audrey, "Now seven presidents have met me."

Despite all of Ted's success, he and Audrey lived simply. They owned one car, a silver Cadillac with "GRINCH" always on the license plates. They answered their own phone. Ted did not give in to joining the computer age, and in fact never even owned an electric typewriter. Rather than spending money on luxuries (even buying a new suit was unusual for Ted), the Geisels gave money to good causes, such as universities and hospitals. They also bought land around them, hoping to help preserve the area from development.

Ted's battle with cancer continued. The tumor in his mouth was not fully destroyed by the implant, and it was soon discovered that the disease was spreading into his throat and neck. Still, he kept a positive attitude about his life. At eighty-two, Ted said, "I surf as much as I always have! I climb Mount Everest as much as I always have!" Of course, he had never done either, so he was not lying. His sense of humor and the love of his fans kept him going. In 1985 Ted was given an honorary degree from Princeton University, and as he stood before the graduating class, all of the students stood up and loudly recited word-for-word the book *Green Eggs and Ham*. Dr. Seuss was deeply touched.

Not one to waste any of his experiences, Ted started writing a book about growing old. *You're Only Old Once* was subtitled *A Book for Obsolete Children*, and made fun of doctors and hospitals, especially the high cost of medical care—things Ted knew a lot about. Although the children's book division worked on the book with Ted, it was the adult division that worked to sell it—to adults, of course. This was Ted's forty-fifth book, and it appeared on his eighty-second birthday in 1986. During a book-signing at a New York bookstore, Ted joked as he looked at the neverending line of 1,300 fans who waited for his signature, "Thank God my name isn't Henry Wadsworth Longfellow!"

Later that year, he and Audrey returned to Springfield, Massachusetts for a Dr. Seuss exhibition and to see his old neighborhood once more. They walked down Mulberry Street, and the townspeople were overjoyed to see their native son return. Two hundred school children greeted him, flying a banner that read: "And to think that we saw him on Mulberry Street!" He held the children's hands and wiped away tears as they recited lines from *Green Eggs and Ham.* Ted took Helen to his old home, where he was welcomed to come inside. He showed his wife the rooms where he had punched pencil holes in the walls and had sketched funny-looking animals on the wallpaper, long since covered over.

By 1987, Ted's health was not good. He kept working, however, this time on a Beginner Book called *I Am Not Going to Get Up Today!* He is only able to work on the words, and has another artist, James Stevenson, do the illustrations. Knowing he was reaching the end of his life, Ted turns his attention to revising some of his older books for future editions. *Mulberry Street* needed the most work because of some racial stereotypes. He had a Chinese man drawn as yellow-skinned with a pigtail hairstyle. "That's the way things were fifty years ago," Ted told people. "In later editions I refer to him as a Chinese man. I have taken the color out of the gentleman and removed the pigtail and now he looks like an

Irishman." One other important change appeared in *The Lorax*. The first edition had included the line "I hear things are just as bad up in Lake Erie." Some scientists who were involved in the cleanup project for Lake Erie actually wrote to Dr. Seuss, asking him if he might consider changing that reference since Lake Erie was now much cleaner. The line was later completely deleted from the book.

Not all requested changes were made, however. Two brothers from New Jersey, David and Bob Grinch, wrote to ask Ted to change the name of the Grinch because they were being harassed. He wrote back, letting the boys know that the Grinch was really a hero because, ". . . . he starts out as a villain, but it's not how you start out that counts. It's what you are at the finish." The Grinch stayed.

Eight-hour workdays continued for Ted. In 1989, he immersed himself in what he knew would be his last book, *Oh the Places You'll Go!* Somehow he had found the strength to both write and illustrate this last book, and in 1990 it became a beloved addition to the Dr. Seuss collection of books.

Over the years at La Jolla, Ted had loved to give away books and autographs to support children's organizations, schools, and zoos. When the San Diego Youth and Community Services group asked for donations for a fund-raising auction, the rock group Aerosmith agreed to send in a signed guitar if Dr. Seuss would donate some autographed books. Ted donated money to some La Jolla High School science students who needed help getting to a Science Olympiad with their project called "The Scrambler." It was used to launch an egg ten meters into a wall, creating a scrambled egg inside. Ted's check arrived

Audrey Geisel stands next to a giant blow up of a Cat in the Hat stamp in 1999 in Springfield, Massachusetts. The United States Post Office issued 15 Cat in the Hat Stamps.

with a note attached: "Scrambling has always been my favorite Olympic sport."

As Ted grew weaker and weaker, his wife, family, and friends gathered around to spend the remaining time with a man they had grown to love. His close friend and chief biographer, Neil Morgan, asked Ted what message he would like to leave behind. His answer: "I always tell myself: 'You can do better than this.' The best slogan I can think of to leave with the U.S.A. would be: 'We can do and we've *got* to do better than this.'" And he was not just talking to children this time. He was talking to everyone.

Ted refused to return to a hospital. He stayed at his home with Audrey, sleeping more and more as days went by. On September 24, 1991 at about 10:00 P.M., Theodor Seuss Geisel died at the age of 87. Nearby was the drawing board that had helped bring Dr. Seuss to the hands of children everywhere.

The Tributes Continue

How did it get so late so soon?
It's night before it's afternoon.
December is here before it's June.
My goodness how the time has flewn.
How did it get so late so soon?

—Dr. Seuss

Theodor Seuss Geisel has no marked grave for fans to visit. Instead, he can be "visited" by sitting with any one of the forty-eight books he created. *Time* magazine honored Dr. Seuss by saying he was "one of the last doctors to make house calls—some 200 million of them in 20 languages." *USA Today* offered these words about the death of Dr. Seuss:

This is no time for fun,
This is no time for play,
Dr. Seuss is no more,
It's a sad, sad, sad day.

Since his death, thousands of pieces of his original work have been donated to universities across the country. Some of these can be seen at the University of California at San Diego and at Los Angeles. Springfield, Massachusetts, Ted's hometown, opened the Dr. Seuss National Memorial in June 2002. Five sculptures created by Audrey Geisel's daughter and Ted's stepdaughter highlight the best of Dr. Seuss's works. These sculptures include Yertle the Turtle in the Yertle Garden, a 14-foot high Horton the elephant in Horton Court, a 4-foot tall Lorax on a tree stump that reads "Unless," and, of course, Dr. Seuss himself at his drawing board with the Cat in the Hat beside him. Random House Books for Young Readers has established a Dr. Seuss Picture Book Award for a first-time author and illustrator, offering a $25,000 prize and a guaranteed book contract in memory of the wonderful work of Ted Geisel, also known as Theo LeSeig, Rosetta Stone, and—best of all—Dr. Seuss.

1904 Theodor Seuss Geisel is born March 2 in Springfield, Massachustetts

1906 Sister Henrietta Geisel born

1907 Sister Henrietta Geisel dies

1918 Meets Theodore Roosevelt in recognition of selling war bonds

1921 Enters Dartmouth College

1925 Graduates Dartmouth College
Goes to England and enters Oxford College
Meets Helen Palmer

1926 Travels Europe with his family

1927 Returns to US
First cartoon published in *Saturday Evening Post*
Moves to New York City
Marries Helen Palmer

1928 Starts work illustrating ads for Flit insecticide

1931 Mother Henrietta Geisel dies

1938 Moves to Random House from Vanguard Press

1941 Moves to Hollywood to join the Signal Corps

1945 Goes to Germany to work on *Your Job in Germany* film
Sister Marnie Geisel dies

1948 Moves to La Jolla, California with Helen

1954 Helen diagnosed with Guillain-Barré Syndrome

1956 Receives honorary doctorate from Dartmouth College

1957 Becomes president of Random House's Beginner Books division

1966 Works on TV adaptation of *How the Grinch Stole Christmas* with
      Chuck Jones
How the Grinch Stole Christmas airs on December 18

1967 Works on TV adaptation of *Horton Hears a Who!*; airs
      on Thanksgiving
Helen Geisel dies

1969 Marries Audrey Stone

1975 Undergoes treatment for glaucoma

1980 Eyesight restored

1983 First diagnosed with cancer; undergoes treatment

1985 Receives honorary degree from Princeton University

1991 Dies on September 24

AND TO THINK THAT I SAW IT ON MULBERRY STREET

HORTON HATCHES THE EGG

HOW THE GRINCH STOLE CHRISTMAS

THE CAT IN THE HAT

YERTLE THE TURTLE

GREEN EGGS AND HAM

THE LORAX

THE BUTTER BATTLE BOOK

OH, THE PLACES YOU'LL GO!

1937 *And to Think That I Saw It on Mulberry Street*

1938 *The 500 Hats of Bartholomew Cubbins*

1939 *The Seven Lady Godivas*
The King's Stilts

1940 *Horton Hatches the Egg*

1947 *McElligot's Pool* (Caldecott Honor Award)

1948 *Thidwick the Big-Hearted Moose*

1949 *Bartholomew and the Oobleck* (Caldecott Honor Award)

1950 *If I Ran the Zoo* (Caldecott Honor Award)

1951 *Gerald McBoing McBoing* (cartoon film) (Academy Award)

1952 *The 5,000 Fingers of Dr. T* (cartoon film)

1953 *Scrambled Eggs Super!*

1954 *Horton Hears a Who!*

1955 *On Beyond Zebra*

1956 *If I Ran the Circus*

1957 *How the Grinch Stole Christmas*
*The Cat in the Hat**

1958 *The Cat in the Hat Comes Back**
Yertle the Turtle and Other Stories

1959 *Happy Birthday to You!*

1960 *Green Eggs and Ham**
*One Fish Two Fish Red Fish Blue Fish**

1961 *The Sneetches and Other Stories*
*Ten Apples Up on Top***

1962 *Dr. Seuss's Sleep Book*

1963 *Hop on Pop**
*Dr. Seuss's ABC**

1965 *Fox in Socks**
I Had Trouble Getting to Solla Sollew
*I Wish I Had Duck Feet***

1966 *Come Over to My House***
How the Grinch Stole Christmas (television special)
        (1972 Peabody Award)

1967 *The Cat in the Hat Song Book*
Horton Hears a Who! (television special) (1972 Peabody Award)

1968 *The Foot Book**
The Eye Book**

1969 *I Can Lick 50 Tigers Today! and Other Stories*
My Book about Me

1970 *I Can Draw It Myself*
Mr. Brown Can Moo! Can You?*

1971 *I Can Write—by Me, Myself***
The Lorax

1972 *In a People House***
Marvin K. Mooney Will You Please Go Now!

1973 *The Many Mice of Mr. Brice***
Did I Ever Tell You How Lucky You Are?
The Shape of Me and Other Stuff*

1974 *There's a Wocket in My Pocket**

1975 *Because a Little Bug Went Ka-Choo!***
Oh, the Thinks You Can Think*
Would You Rather Be a Bullfrog?**

1976 *Hooper Humperdink...? Not Him!***
The Cat's Quizzer*

1977 *Try to Remember the First of Octember***
Halloween Is Grinch Night (television special) (Emmy Award)

1978 *I Can Read with My Eyes Shut!**

1979 *Oh, Say Can You Say?**

1980 *Maybe You Should Fly a Jet! Maybe You Should Be a Vet!***

1981 *The Tooth Book***

1982 *Hunches in Bunches*
The Grinch Grinches the Cat in the Hat (television special)
(Emmy Award)

1984 *The Butter Battle Book*

1986 *You're Only Old Once!*

1987 *I Am Not Going to Get Up Today!**

1990 *Oh, The Places You'll Go*

Posthumous Publications

1991   *Six by Seuss: A Treasury of Dr. Seuss Classics*

1995   *Daisy-Head Mayzie*
       The Secret Art of Dr. Seuss

1996   *My Many-Colored Days*
       A Hatful of Seuss

1997   *Seuss-isms: Wise and Witty Prescriptions for Living from the
       Good Doctor*

1998   *Hooray for Diffendoofer Day* (completed by Jack Prelutsky
       using Ted Geisel's notes)

* indicates a Beginner or Bright & Early Book
** indicates a Theo LeSeig or other pseudonym used

MAD MARY lives in the woods with vultures for watchdogs? Mary is a fascinating character who makes a tasty road kill stew and has boxes of books lining her cozy cave. She rejected society after her wealthy father's home burned down around him, and while she's a definitely eccentric, the only thing "mad" about her is her name.

THE CAT IN THE HAT is the sly character who mysteriously appears one day and entertains two kids with his "tricks" and "games," though their fish is suspicious of the Cat's intentions.

HORTON is the elephant who takes it upon himself to hatch an egg he sees in a tree.

THE GRINCH is Dr. Seuss' own Ebeneezer Scrooge who tries to ruin Christmas for the town of Whoville by stealing all their gifts—only to discover that the town still celebrates as happily as they would have even if their presents weren't stolen.

THE LORAX tries to save the Truffula Forest from the Once-ler's greedy actions.

YERTLE THE TURTLE lives in a society where the king insists on standing on the shoulders of his subjects. Yertle is at the bottom of this pile and doesn't want to stay there.

SAM-I-AM is the persistent character who wants a grumpy man to eat green eggs and ham . . . until finally the man agrees and discovers he actually likes them.

1946   Academy Award, Best Documentary Feature, *Your Job in Germany*

1947   Academy Award, Best Documentary Feature, *Design for Death*

1951   Academy Award, Best Animated Cartoon, *Gerald McBoing McBoing*

1972   Peabody Award, *How the Grinch Stole Christman*
Peabody Award, *Horton Hears a Who!*
Critics Award, International Animated Cartoon Festival, *The Lorax*
Silver Medal, International Film and TV Festival of New York,
    Dr. Seuss on the Loose

1974   Los Angeles County Library Association Award

1976   Outstanding California Author Award, California Assoc. of
    Teachers of English

1977   Emmy Award, *Halloween Is Grinch Night*

1980   Laura Ingalls Wilder Award, American Library Association

1982   Regina Medal, Catholic Library Association
Special Award for Distinguished Service to Children, National
    Assoc. of Elementary School Principals
Emmy Award, *The Grinch Grinches the Cat in the Hat*

1984   Pulitzer Prize

1986   New York Public Library Literary Lion

Bandler, Michael J. "Seuss on the Loose," *Parents*. September 1987.

WEBSITES

http://www.randomhouse.com/seussville/
  [Seussville, the official Dr. Seuss website from Random House.]

PICTURE CREDITS

page:

6: Associated Press, AP

10: Associated Press, AP

14: Associated Press, AP

16: Corbis

22: Associated Press, AP

25: Not selected yet

28: Hulton Archive by
Getty Images

35: Hulton Archive by
Getty Images

40: Hulton Archive by
Getty Images

46: Hulton Archive by
Getty Images

50: Hulton Archive by
Getty Images

57: Hulton Archive by
Getty Images

62: Hulton Archive by
Getty Images

68: Hulton Archive by
Getty Images

74: Hulton Archive by
Getty Images

76: Hulton Archive by
Getty Images

82: Hulton Archive by
Getty Images

88: Hulton Archive by
Getty Images

92: Hulton Archive by
Getty Images

97: Hulton Archive by
Getty Images

cover: Associated Press, AP

TANYA DEAN is a children's book writer, editor, agent, and conference speaker. She taught history and English for twelve years before moving into the field of publishing. Ms. Dean was vice-president and publisher of Willowisp Press/Pages Publishing Group, a children's book-fair publishing company. She was also the managing editor of a nationally known teen magazine. These days, Ms. Dean is an executive editor at SRA/McGraw-Hill where she is responsible for the development of elementary reading materials. This is Ms. Dean's eighteenth book.

8/0